D1643680

PICTURESQUE OLD EDINBURGH
EXTRA-ILLUSTRATED EDITION

White Horse Close

John Knox's House

PICTURESQUE OLD EDINBURGH

By

ROBERT LOUIS STEVENSON

Preface by
JEAN DESEBROCK, B. Litt.

Illustrated by
HERBERT RAILTON
and Others

EDINBURGH : ALBYN PRESS LTD
CHARLES SKILTON PUBLISHING GROUP

© Albyn Press Ltd 1983
in respect of new material
and illustration layout

Made and printed
in Great Britain by
The Garden City Press Ltd
Letchworth, Herts.
from typesetting by
Alacrity Phototypesetters
Banwell Castle, Weston-super-Mare
and published by
ALBYN PRESS LTD
2, 3 & 4 Abbeymount
Edinburgh 8

PREFACE

By Jean Desebrock, B. Litt. (Oxon.)

One's native city can be an awkward thing to come to terms with, to see without prejudice: one's apprehension of it is so coloured by personal experience, and the taste of one's past life is so often the taste of the place that was its stage. Yet none can know a place and its atmosphere as the native of it does. When a great writer paints in words the portrait of a great city which is his own there is a special interest. Robert Louis Stevenson's *Picturesque Old Edinburgh* (originally published as *Edinburgh: Picturesque Notes*) has been called by Francis Watt 'the gem of all books on Edinburgh'.

Edinburgh, a dramatic city of extremes, has had a more powerful influence on its people than most native cities; it seems to penetrate sensitive growing minds with a strange intensity. The mind of the young Robert Louis Stevenson, who spent his childhood, adolescence and early manhood in Edinburgh, was one of the most interesting to be so indelibly imprinted. In the years after he had left his city and country, early impressions were constantly to flood back to him — pleasant childhood memories first gathered through the genteel windows of 17 Heriot Row, and, later, sharper insights brought together during the painful and stormy adolescence of a discontented and rebellious youth. During these latter days, leaning on the parapet of the North Bridge, he would watch, longingly, as trains busied away 'on a voyage to brighter skies. Happy the passengers', he would muse, 'who shake off the dust of Edinburgh, and have heard for the last time the cry of the east wind among her chimney tops. And yet the place,' he adds, 'establishes an interest in people's hearts; go where they will, they find no city of the same distinction; go where they will, they take a pride in their old home.'

The young rebel felt chained and trammelled in his city, though his complaints were due more, perhaps, to the natural perversity of youth than to the oppressiveness of the place. It is common enough for the restless and intelligent adolescent to rebel against the city of his youth, to revile it and feel enclosed by it. It does not mean that, in the end, a place as memorable as Edinburgh could be forgotten. Indeed, no sooner had Stevenson escaped from it than, ironically, he retreated to France and wrote about the city he had, most of his life, longed to leave. His book on Edinburgh was written in Monastier in 1878. Stevenson never drew his home country and countrymen more clearly than when he was away from them.

Perhaps not surprisingly, Stevenson's attitude to Edinburgh as expressed in *Picturesque Old Edinburgh*, written after he had freed himself from its bonds, is still ambivalent. He wrote his best of his strong loves and hates, and when he wrote of Edinburgh he was torn between the two: amidst an inescapable pride he expresses the scars of revulsion. After opening the book with words of praise for the city's splendid setting, he promptly goes on to complain how cruelly she pays for it with 'one of the vilest climates under heaven'. Yet, in other words of his, 'No place so brands a man...' and inextricably bound up with memories of personal youth he carried the feeling of his city with him always:

> Do you remember — can we e'er forget?
> How, in the coiled perplexities of youth,
> In our wild climate, in our scowling town,
> We gloomed and shivered, sorrowed, sobbed and feared!...
>
> Yet when the lamp from my expiring eyes
> Shall dwindle and recede, the voice of love
> Fall insignificant on my closing ears,
> What sound shall come but the old cry of the wind
> In our inclement city?

The terrible climate of Edinburgh was what he hated most about it and what he, in his delicate state of health, suffered from more than most. He would constantly recall the place, with its dominant jagged rock and hills — 'precipitous' was one of his favourite words to describe it — and would recall also the pain of the cold, cold winds which blasted his frail lungs. In one of the very last poems he wrote the scene is still in his mind:

> ...Hearkening I heard again
> In my precipitous city beaten bells
> Winnow the keen sea wind...

Picturesque Old Edinburgh, generically a long essay but first published in the *Portfolio* in six parts before appearing in book form, builds up an emotive and superbly evocative picture of the city. Stevenson's great talent here is for the recreation of atmosphere: what Edinburgh *feels* like breathes through his pages as the life of places seldom does through passages describing them. It is not a guide book; it is a unique collection of personal reflections from one who knew his city thoroughly in all her guises, written with the guarded affection of one seeing all too well. Edinburgh is a strangely immutable city, standing firmly on a natural stage and less a fool of time than most. Partly for this reason, and because a good book says something new to each generation, *Picturesque Old Edinburgh* has held its relevance and interest: it remains today one of the finest and truest accounts of the city. It recalls like no other book does what Edinburgh looks like, and *is* like.

Stevenson's carefully tutored prose, charming, enthusiastic, sometimes over mannered, has, in a shoddier modern world, lost none of its effect. A contemporary critic described it succinctly in the *Saturday Review*: 'It speaks for itself; it is captivating and irritating; it keeps the attention awake; it sketches in pictures; in two words, it is never commonplace; it retains an accent of the quaintness of a time of leisure.'

*   *   *

Robert Louis Stevenson (1850-94) spent the first twenty-five years of his life in Edinburgh, years that fall into two quite distinct periods: happy childhood and troubled youth. By the age of twenty-five he had won through to a greater stability: the rebel had rebelled. But now his native city was set behind him.

He was born, on November 13th, 1850, at 8 Howard Place, Edinburgh, of a family long of Edinburgh. His father, Thomas Stevenson, a well-to-do, well situated, strictly Presbyterian businessman, joint-engineer to the Board of Northern Lighthouses, was a kindly but conventional and, in some ways, aloof figure. His mother was a minister's daughter, of pleasantly bouyant character, with a great fund of optimism, inherited by her son. It was after her father, the Rev. Dr Lewis Balfour, that her son was named, being christened Robert Lewis Balfour Stevenson. The story behind the change in the spelling (but not the pronunciation) of his name Lewis to the French form is that Mr Stevenson feared that a relationship by marriage would be suspected between his family and that of a vocal young Radical town councillor by the name of Lewis, whom he, a staunch Conservative, regarded with the utmost aversion.

The small neat house in which Stevenson's life began was, in 1850, on the northern outskirts of Edinburgh, the very fringe of the New Town. Along the road to the Forth stood fine old country houses with large parks, and facing Louis's first home was the black ridge of Corstorphine Hill, in those days not shut out by the houses which were soon to hem Howard Place in on all sides.

The sickly little boy, an only, treasured, sunny-natured child, reared in a comfortable home, enjoyed a childhood of rare happiness, lapped as he was in the love of his parents and the immortal 'Cummy', Alison Cunningham, his nurse and second mother, who joined the family when he was eighteen months old. Cummy nurtured the tender little plant in her care with a love he treasured all his life. Even in his long and frequent periods of illness he experienced such contentment that he could later look back on them as 'pleasant', thanks to the cheerful patience of his mother and nurse. Petted and surrounded by admiring adults, he was the lord of his house; all his whims were gratified; but though the delicate little boy was of necessity greatly protected, he was never a spoilt child.

A neighbour recollected seeing young Lou, or 'Smout' as he was then called, being taken on his first walks from the house in Howard Place, being led gently along the sunniest side of the pavement, firmly clasping his nurse's hand, his face swathed in flannel to alleviate earache. Cummy would lift him up when they crossed Canonmills Bridge so that he could look over the parapet and watch the Water of Leith as it swirled down in winter, a turbulent flood overflowing its channel. Cummy remained with the family till Louis was grown up and the family was parted by travels, marriages and deaths. To her he was always 'my laddie'. Her influence on him cannot be overestimated: through her he was weaned on Calvinism and a rich world of wonderful stories; in later life he could not think of Edinburgh without thinking of Cummy.

Cummy's own recollections of a petticoated little boy of three or four suggest that his desire to write was born at a tender time of life. She told of an eager small hand being slid into hers, with earnest signals to lock the door and maintain the utmost secrecy. 'I've got a story to tell, Cummy — you write it!' in an excited stage whisper. 'I wrote down every word he told me,' she recalled.

Within a few years the business enterprises of Thomas Stevenson had so prospered that the family moved to 17 Heriot Row in what is still one of the finest streets in the urbane and stately New Town. There Louis spent the most impressionable years of his childhood and there gathered his first real memories of Edinburgh through the big windows overlooking private gardens and the 'lamp before the door', lit magically each evening by the envied lamplighter. During continued weary nights of illness the surrounding town became important to him.

> Nothing but lamps the whole town through,
> And never a child awake but you

he wrote in 'The Sick Child'. In 'Nuits Boanches', an early paper, he recalled 'the sickly child that woke from his few hours' slumber with the sweat of a nightmare on his brow, to lie awake,

17 Heriot Row

and listen, and long for the first signs of life among the silent streets. Over the black belt of the garden I saw the long line of Queen Street, with here and there a lighted window. How often my nurse lifted me out of bed and pointed them out to me, while we wondered together if, there also, there were children that could not sleep, and if these lighted oblongs were signs of those that waited, like us, for the morning.'

Not till he was eight or more did Louis learn to read for himself, a failure both compensated for and due to the fact that his mother and Cummy were all too willing to entertain him with reading aloud. He would prance about in high excitement as marvellous adventures were retailed: chairs became heroes, the coal box a castle holding captives, the table an enchanted island, as fights were fought out against pillows till his elders were alarmed at his breathlessness.

Cummy's readings from the Bible (she claimed to have read it through to him three or four times before he could read for himself, but perhaps it only felt like it), from *Pilgrim's Progress* and *Fox's Book of Martyrs* seem to have appealed to the inquisitive young imagination as much as children's story-books. Through the sleepless nights and days of his illnesses, toys spread around him, toy soldiers marching among the bedclothes, 'Cummy, read to me from the Bible,' he would demand when he could not sleep. But more even than this he loved Cummy's own narrations.

The sickly child's schooling was, to say the least, intermittent, his father setting more store by his son's health than his assimilation of anything schoolmasters could teach him. Even after his schooldays began when he was eight years old he continued to learn far more at home than at school. Watching other children going to school, he had been anxious to join them, but his interest soon died once he found how difficult it was to be accepted by his robust and often cruel classmates, who did not wish to know about the imaginative games he liked to invent or listen to the precocious chatter that so amused his elders. Noticing how Cummy would walk him to school and see that he 'changed his feet' for fear of a chill, they would jeer at the sensitive boy whose secure little world had hitherto not included criticism.

Before starting school he had had little contact with other children. He did have cousins, however, who were more sympathetic to his imagination, and did not mind being organised into opposing armies or playing the game of 'islands', inventing their own little worlds. Still, his best games did not need to be

*Stevenson bought his
toy theatres at the shop
on the left*

shared. One of his early passions was for toy theatres, for which a grand selection of sheets of paper characters and scenery could be bought, cut out and brought to life by a lively imagination. His later celebrated essay, 'Penny Plain, Twopence Coloured', recalled these and the shop which sold them. 'There stands, I fancy, to this day,' he wrote, 'a certain stationers shop at a corner of the wide thoroughfare that joins the city of my childhood to the sea...' (Leith Walk; the shop still stands there, at the corner of Antigua Street, though not now a stationers and newsagents) where bloodcurdling 'budgets of romance' lay in a pile. On a Saturday, clutching his week's pocket money, he would linger at the old bow window where 'all the year round there stood displayed a theatre in working order', with a 'forest set', a 'combat', and a few 'robbers carousing in the slides'. He recalled the eager but cautious child so slow to make up his mind in the little shop, where it was 'dark, and smelt of Bibles', that the impatience of the owner was kindled. At last he would gather up his chosen penny plains and hurry home to paint them.

Early childhood summers frequently took him to Colinton, just outside Edinburgh, where his grandfather's manse garden, a wooded private playground with the Water of Leith at its foot, fitted snugly under the Pentland Hills. Cummy recalled days 'like green spots in my memory' when his mother loved to see him running in the garden of her own childhood, in temporary good health. In his later boyhood he travelled much, following a kinder sun. There were visits to England and the South of France, experiences which, with his wide reading, were to keep him unusually free from insular prejudices. He began also to interest himself in his own city. 'The memories of an Edinburgh boy are partly the memories of the town,' he was later to write. 'I look back with delight on many an escalade of garden walls, many a ramble among lilacs full of piping birds, many an exploration in obscure quarters that were neither town nor country.'

In 1863 Stevenson was enrolled at the Edinburgh Academy and spent a few interrupted terms there, still making few friends. Yet these solitary schoolboy days were a seed time for what was later to be a rich harvest of ideas. Eventually, between 1864 and 1867, he attended a little school run by a Mr Thomson which had only about a dozen pupils and where the light tasks suited his ill-health and left him valuable time for literary pursuits.

So drew to an end the first half of Stevenson's life in Edinburgh: that of a secure, happy, though at times solitary, boyhood, a life moulded by the cheerful precept: 'Be good yourself, make others happy.' He was then contented, unthinkingly, to accept social norms and the world as he found it. He had not yet quite outgrown the happy show child who, dressed up for a social occasion by loving adult hands, would delight all with his frank and courteous manners, his desire to please and be pleased.

The sensitive adolescent began, however, to feel incarcerated within the prison of civilization. It greatly galled him: feeling fettered and separate, he began writing earnestly. In 1867 his easy-going schooldays ended. That same year, when he was seventeen, his parents leased Swanston Cottage, a secluded and substantial country house a few miles from the city, in 'a green fold in the lap of the Pentlands', sheltered from the cold winds blowing off the sea. Here he befriended the booming-voiced shepherd John Todd who, in rich Scottish dialect, recounted wonderful tales of stirring times. 'He was a wayfarer,' said Stevenson, 'and took my gipsy fancy.'

Stevenson now entered Edinburgh University, at first study-
ing engineering: he would, his father earnestly hoped, follow the
family tradition and become a lighthouse engineer. Stevenson
later described himself at this time as 'a certain lean, ugly, idle,
unpopular student, full of changing humours, fine occasional
purposes of good, unflinching acceptance of evil, shiverings on
wet east-windy mornings, journeys up to class, infinite yawnings
during lectures, and unquestionable gusto in the delights of
truantry.' His friend Baildon, whom he met in his last years at
school, while not agreeing to call him 'ugly', agrees that 'In body
he was assuredly badly set up. His limbs were long, lean and
spidery, and his chest flat, so as almost to suggest malnutriment,
such sharp corners did his joints make under his clothes.'
Another student contemporary of Stevenson's, writing in a daily
newspaper on the occasion of Stevenson's death, describes him as
'a thin, pale-faced youth, with piercing eyes, ever in a hurry,
cigarette in mouth and muffler round his neck, and with loose
locks which suggested an advisable early interview with a skilful
barber.'

This much discussed 'Bohemian' period of Stevenson's life was
one of profound revolt and uncertainly. The cultivated oddities
of behaviour and looks, the long hair, shabby velvet jacket and
eccentric clothes, aimed to outrage and provoke attention. At
this time Stevenson began to discover a side to Edinburgh which
was far from the middle-class drawing rooms of his sheltered
childhood. The contrasts between respectable Edinburgh and its
underworld were great, and yet the areas in which each flourished
were in close proximity. Stevenson now discovered, in a mood of
perverse delight, the underworld howffs around Leith, the
Calton Hill and the Old Town, and the colourful haunts of the
seamen of Leith, of thieves and prostitutes, revealing a whole new
undiscovered world perfect for one in revolt against an over-
bearing establishment. Contrasts, he found, abounded in Edinburgh, and the rebellious student loved contrasts. He found,
however, more than a world of mud to be set beside the pompous
and opinionated respectable world, he found people who would
accept a man for what he was and not question it. His own class

The West Bow

mocked him for an affected fool; the underworld tolerated.

Details of actual companions and doings are scarce, though there is some evidence to suggest his love for a 'fallen' girl in or on the fringes of this second Edinburgh. He later wrote a novel *Claire*, the story of a streetwalker, which was deliberately destroyed. Other hints remain in semi-private writings, such as the chivalrous and protective attitude to women expressed in a letter to a young art student: 'Whatever you do, see that you don't sacrifice a woman; that is where all imperfect loves conduct us. At the same time (if you can make it convenient to be chaste) for God's sake avoid the primness of your virtue. Hardness to a poor harlot is a sin lower than the ugliest unchastity.' And the poignant little verse:

· 15 ·

God gave to me a child in part,
Yet wholly gave the father's heart:
Child of my soul, O wither now
Unborn, unmothered, goest thou?

Stevenson's feeling for his parents, despite the strains of his student years, seems always to have retained the intensity bequeathed by a happy childhood. His relationship with his father, made uneasy by antagonisms of temperament, was nevertheless close. Flora Masson*, recalling a dinner party at the Stevenson house in Heriot Row, draws a sharp picture of father and son:

Father and son both talked, taking diametrically opposite points of view on all things under the sun. Mr Stevenson seemed to me, on that evening, to be the type of the kindly, orthodox Edinburgh father... But Louis Stevenson, on my other side, was on that evening in one of his most recklessly brilliant moods. His talk was almost incessant. I remember feeling quite dazed at the amount of intellection he expended on each subject, however trivial in itself, that he touched upon. He worried it, as a dog might worry a rat, and then threw it off lightly, as some chance word or allusion set him thinking, and talking, of something else. The father's face at certain moments was a study — an indescribable mixture of vexation, fatherly pride and admiration, and sheer bewilderment at the boy's brilliant flippancies, and the quick young thrusts of his wit and criticism.

Stevenson, despite his solitariness, was at this time one of the brightest lights in a brilliant university coterie, and a keen actor in amateur theatricals.

At the end of one of those performances of *Twelfth Night* [in which Stevenson had played Orsino], when the audience was thronging into the hall, and the carriages were being called at the front door in stentorian tones, we saw Louis Stevenson's mother making her way out alone, her pretty face still radiant with maternal pride. Louis Stevenson... was looking down over the balustrade, half-way up the staircase. But in a moment he was down among the departing guests; wrapped his mother's cloak with an infinite tenderness about her, and then, escaping from the crowd's admiring eyes, fled up the staircase again. I can still see the upward look of adoration his mother gave him, as she went on her way among the departing guests, triumphant.†

* *I Can Remember Robert Louis Stevenson*, ed. Rosaline Masson, Chambers, Edinburgh, 1922.

† *Ibid.*

Thomas Stevenson was deeply wounded by his son's reluctance to pursue his profession, by his Bohemianism and, most profoundly, by his rejection of his creed. His son, it seemed, was becoming a social outcast, uninterested in most orthodox entertainments and unwilling to mix with his equals in social standing. Wayward and impatient, he was full of the gloom of youth. In a letter he later recorded his own terse summary of this period of his life: 'I was educated for a civil engineer on my father's design, and was at the building of harbours and lighthouses, and worked in a carpenter's shop and a brass foundry, and hung about wood-yards and the like. Then it came out I was learning nothing, and, on being tightly cross-questioned during a dreadful evening walk, I owned I cared for nothing but literature. My father said that was no profession, but I might be called to the Bar if I chose. At the age of twenty-one I began to study law.'

Though his heart was not in it, he bravely persevered at his legal studies, leaving time for other reading and writing. He did not care for outdoor pursuits: 'Life', he noted, 'does not appear to me to be an amusement adapted to this weather.' The wintry days of Edinburgh greatly depressed him; nights seemed preferable, when the lamps seemed to shine on the rainy streets more warmly than the weak sun. He was now writing seriously. 'No-one ever had such pains to learn a trade as I had,' he later admitted, 'but I slogged at it day in day out, and I frankly believe (thanks to my dire industry) I have done more with smaller gifts than almost any man of letters in the world.' The seeming idler was in reality always busy, always armed with two books, one to read and one to write in. 'It was not so much that I wished to be an author... as that I vowed that I would *learn to write*... I practised to acquire it, as men learn to whistle, in a wager with myself.'

In 1875 the door plate engraved 'R.L. Stevenson, Advocate' went up in Heriot Row, but his search for hire in this field was never seriously pursued; eventually gown and wig were abandoned altogether. By this time Stevenson, on the point of leaving Edinburgh, was free at last to make his break. The man that had emerged from the troubled boy was more relaxed and confident.

He is described at this time as an excellent talker by a winter fireside who could change in a moment from grave to cheerful, never ceasing to entertain.

In his later, though short, life, Robert Louis Stevenson's travels took him to Europe and then to California where — a final statement of independence — he married Mrs Osbourne, a divorcee, in 1880. After a stay at Calistoga he returned to Britain, very ill, but his undiminished literary output now brought him fame. Before sailing, in 1888, for the South Seas and settling in Samoa, where he was to die suddenly from a ruptured blood-vessel in the brain in 1894, he paid his final visit the previous year to Edinburgh. One of the last people to see him there was Flora Masson:

> An open cab, with a man and woman in it, seated side by side, and leaning back — the rest of the cab piled high with rather untidy luggage — came slowly towards us, westward, along Princes Street. It was evidently carrying travellers to the railway station. As it passed us, out on the broad roadway . . . a slender, loose-garbed figure stood up in the cab and waved a wide-brimmed hat.
>
> 'Good-bye!' he called to us. 'Good-bye!'
>
> 'It is Louis Stevenson!' said my companion; 'they must be going away again.'
>
> Was this the Louis Stevenson of the 'Seventies, the boy who played truant from the college classes, the 'queer, lank lad in a velvet coat' whose brilliant talk had so perplexed and charmed us?
>
> This figure, standing up in the open cab, waving the wide-brimmed hat, was an older man, an invalid, a wanderer; a man who had felt warmer sun's rays than ever warm Edinburgh stones, and had, I am sure, battled with harder winds than ever blow in Edinburgh. This was Louis Stevenson, the brilliant and distinguished Man of Letters of whom his native City was very proud.
>
> The cab passed. The gray vista of our Northern Capital, the long line of Princes Street, was at its very best as Louis Stevenson looked back at it and us, over the back of the open cab, still waving his hat and calling 'Good-bye!' That little bit of west-endy, east-windy Edinburgh, with the gray and green of the Castle Rock and the gardens on the one side, and Princes Street itself, glittering in the sunshine, on the other! It was Edinburgh's last sight of Louis Stevenson, and Louis Stevenson's last look back at the City that was his birthplace, in which he had been so happy and so miserable; that he had chafed against and railed at; that he was to write about and dream about in exile, and to love immeasurably to the end.*

* Flora Masson, *Ibid.*

INTRODUCTORY

THE ANCIENT and famous metropolis of the North sits overlooking a windy estuary from the slope and summit of three hills. No situation could be more commanding for the head city of a kingdom; none better chosen for noble prospects. From her tall precipice and terraced gardens she looks far and wide on the sea and broad champaigns. To the east you may catch at sunset the spark of the May lighthouse, where the Firth expands into the German Ocean; and away to the west, over all the carse of Stirling, you can see the first snows upon Ben Ledi.

But Edinburgh pays cruelly for her high seat in one of the vilest climates under heaven. She is liable to be beaten upon by all the winds that blow, to be drenched with rain, to be buried in cold sea fogs out of the east, and powdered with the snow as it comes flying southward from the Highland hills. The weather is raw and boisterous in winter, shifty and ungenial in summer, and a downright meteorological purgatory in the spring. The delicate die early, and I, as a survivor, among bleak winds and plumping rain, have been sometimes tempted to envy them their fate. For all who love shelter and the blessings of the sun, who hate dark weather and perpetual tilting against squalls, there could scarcely be found a more unhomely and harassing place of residence. Many such aspire angrily after that Somewhere-else of the

The Mound and Castle from North Bridge

imagination, where all troubles are supposed to end. They lean
over the great bridge which joins the New Town with the Old —
that windiest spot, or high altar, in this northern temple of the
winds — and watch the trains smoking out from under them and
vanishing into the tunnel on a voyage to brighter skies. Happy
the passengers who shake off the dust of Edinburgh, and have
heard for the last time the cry of the east wind among her
chimney-tops! And yet the place establishes an interest in
people's hearts; go where they will, they find no city of the same
distinction; go where they will, they take a pride in their old
home.

Venice, it has been said, differs from all other cities in the
sentiment which she inspires. The rest may have admirers; she
only, a famous fair one, counts lovers in her train. And indeed,
even by her kindest friends, Edinburgh is not considered in a
similar sense. These like her for many reasons, not any one of
which is satisfactory in itself. They like her whimsically, if you
will, and somewhat as a virtuoso dotes upon his cabinet. Her
attraction is romantic in the narrowest meaning of the term.
Beautiful as she is, she is not so much beautiful as interesting. She
is pre-eminently Gothic, and all the more so since she has set
herself off with some Greek airs and erected classic temples on
her crags. In a word, and above all, she is a curiosity. The Palace of
Holyrood has been left aside in the growth of Edinburgh, and
stands gray and silent in a workman's quarter and among

Holyrood and Arthur's Seat from Calton Hill

breweries and gas works. It is a house of many memories. Great people of yore, kings and queens, buffoons and grave ambassadors, played their stately farce for centuries in Holyrood. Wars have been plotted, dancing has lasted deep into the night, murder has been done in its chambers. There Prince Charlie held his phantom levées, and in a very gallant manner represented a fallen dynasty for some hours. Now, all these things of clay are mingled with the dust, the king's crown itself is shown for sixpence to the vulgar; but the stone palace has outlived these changes. For fifty weeks together, it is no more than a show for tourists and a museum of old furniture; but on the fifty-first, behold the palace reawakened and mimicking its past. The Lord Commissioner, a kind of stage sovereign, sits among the stage courtiers; a coach and six and clattering escort come and go before the gate; at night, the windows are lighted up, and its near neighbours, the workmen, may dance in their own houses to the palace music. And in this the palace is typical. There is a spark among the embers; from time to time the old volcano smokes. Edinburgh has but partly abdicated, and still wears, in parody, her metropolitan trappings. Half a capital and half a country town, the whole city leads a double existence; it has long trances of the one and flashes of the other; like the king of the Black Isles, it is half alive and half a monumental marble. There are armed men and cannon in the citadel overhead; you may see the troops marshalled on the high parade; and at night after the early winter evenfall, and in the morning before the laggard winter dawn, the wind carries abroad over Edinburgh the sound of drums and bugles. Grave judges sit bewigged in what was once the scene of imperial deliberations. Close by in the High Street perhaps the trumpets may sound about the stroke of noon; and you see a troop of citizens in tawdry masquerade; tabard above, heather-mixture trowser below, and the men themselves trudging in the mud among unsympathetic bystanders. The grooms of a well-appointed circus tread the streets with a better presence. And yet these are the Heralds and Pursuivants of Scotland, who are about to proclaim a new law of the United Kingdom before two score boys, and thieves, and hackney-coachmen. Meanwhile every hour

A Royal
Proclamation

the bell of the University rings out over the hum of the streets, and every hour a double tide of students, coming and going, fills the deep archways. And lastly, one night in the springtime — or say one morning rather, at the peep of day — late folk may hear the voices of many men singing a psalm in unison from a church on one side of the old High Street; and a little after, or perhaps a little before, the sound of many men singing a psalm in unison from another church on the opposite side of the way. There will be something in the words about the dew of Hermon, and how goodly it is to see brethren dwelling together in unity. And the late folk will tell themselves that all this singing denotes the conclusion of two yearly ecclesiastical parliaments — the parliaments of Churches which are brothers in many admirable virtues, but not specially like brothers in this particular of a tolerant and peaceful life.

Again, meditative people will find a charm in a certain consonancy between the aspect of the city and its odd and stirring history. Few places, if any, offer a more barbaric display of contrasts to the eye. In the very midst one of the most satisfactory crags in nature — a Bass Rock upon dry land, rooted in a garden, shaken by passing trains, carrying a crown of battlements and turrets, and describing its warlike shadow over the liveliest and brightest thoroughfare of the new town. From their smoky beehives, ten stories high, the unwashed look down upon the open squares and gardens of the wealthy; and gay people sunning themselves along Princes Street, with its mile of commercial palaces all beflagged upon some great occasion, see, across a gardened valley set with statues, where the washings of the old town flutter in the breeze at its high windows. And then, upon all sides, what a clashing of architecture! In this one valley, where the life of the town goes most busily forward, there may be seen, shown one above and behind another by the accidents of the ground, buildings in almost every style upon the globe. Egyptian and Greek temples, Venetian palaces and Gothic spires, are huddled one over another in a most admired disorder; while, above all, the brute mass of the Castle and the summit of Arthur's Seat look down upon these imitations with a becoming

The Old Town, from East Princes Street Gardens

dignity, as the works of Nature may look down upon the monuments of Art. But Nature is a more indiscriminate patroness than we imagine, and in no way frightened of a strong effect. The birds roost as willingly among the Corinthian capitals as in the crannies of the crag; the same atmosphere and daylight clothe the eternal rock and yesterday's imitation portico; and as the soft northern sunshine throws out everything into a glorified distinctness — or easterly mists, coming up with the blue evening, fuse all these incongruous features into one, and the lamps begin to glitter along the street, and faint lights to burn in the high windows across the valley — the feeling grows upon you that this also is a piece of nature in the most intimate sense; that this profusion of eccentricities, this dream in masonry and living rock, is not a drop-scene in a theatre, but a city in the world of every-day reality, connected by railway and telegraph-wire with all the capitals of Europe, and inhabited by citizens of the familiar type, who keep ledgers, and attend church, and have sold their immortal portion to a daily paper. By all the canons of romance, the place demands to be half deserted and leaning towards decay;

birds we might admit in profusion, the play of the sun and winds, and a few gipsies encamped in the chief thoroughfare: but these citizens, with their cabs and tramways, their trains and posters, are altogether out of key. Chartered tourists, they make free with historic localities, and rear their young among the most picturesque sites with a grand human indifference. To see them thronging by, in their neat clothes and conscious moral rectitude, and with a little air of possession that verges on the absurd, is not the least striking feature of the place.*

And the story of the town is as eccentric as its appearance. For centuries it was a capital thatched with heather, and more than once, in the evil days of English invasion, it has gone up in flame to heaven a beacon to ships at sea. It was the jousting-ground of jealous nobles, not only on Greenside or by the King's Stables, where set tournaments were fought to the sound of trumpets and under the authority of the royal presence, but in every alley where there was room to cross swords, and in the main street, where popular tumult under the Blue Blanket alternated with the brawls of outlandish clansmen and retainers. Down in the palace John Knox reproved his queen in the accents of modern democracy. In the town, in one of those little shops plastered like so many swallows' nests among the buttresses of the old Cathedral, that familiar autocrat, James VI, would gladly share a bottle of wine with George Heriot the goldsmith. Up on the Pentland Hills, that so quietly look down on the Castle with the city lying in waves around it, those mad and dismal fanatics, the

---

* These sentences have, I hear, given offence in my native town, and a proportionable pleasure to our rivals of Glasgow. I confess the news caused me both pain and merriment. May I remark, as a balm for wounded fellow-townsmen, that there is nothing deadly in my accusations? Small blame to them if they keep ledgers: 'tis an excellent business habit. Churchgoing is not, that ever I heard, a subject of reproach; decency of linen is a mark of prosperous affairs, and conscious moral rectitude one of the tokens of good living. It is not their fault if the city calls for something more specious by way of inhabitants. A man in a frock-coat looks out of place upon an Alp or Pyramid, although he has the virtues of a Peabody and the talents of a Bentham. And let them console themselves — they do as well as anybody else; the population of (let us say) Chicago would cut quite as rueful a figure on the same romantic stage. To the Glasgow people I would say only one word, but that is of gold: *I have not yet written a book about Glasgow.*

Sweet Singers, haggard from long exposure on the moors, sat day and night with 'tearful psalms' to see Edinburgh consumed with fire from heaven, like another Sodom or Gomorrah. There, in the Grass-market, stiff-necked, covenanting heroes, offered up the often unnecessary, but not less honourable, sacrifice of their lives, and bade eloquent farewell to sun, moon, and stars, and earthly friendships, or died silent to the roll of drums. Down by yon outlet rode Grahame of Claverhouse and his thirty dragoons, with the town beating to arms behind their horses' tails — a sorry handful thus riding for their lives, but with a man at the head who was to return in a different temper, make a dash that staggered Scotland to the heart, and die happily in the thick of fight. There Aikenhead was hanged for a piece of boyish incredulity; there, a few years afterwards, David Hume ruined Philosophy and Faith, an undisturbed and well-reputed citizen; and thither, in yet a few years more, Burns came from the plough-tail, as to an academy of gilt unbelief and artificial letters. There when the great exodus was made across the valley, and the new town began to spread abroad its draughty parallelograms and rear its long frontage on the opposing hill, there was such a flitting, such a change of domicile and dweller, as was never excelled in the history of cities: the cobbler succeeded the earl; the beggar ensconced himself by the judge's chimney; what had been a palace was used as a pauper refuge; and great mansions were so parcelled out among the least and lowest in society, that the hearthstone of the old proprietor was thought large enough to be partitioned off into a bedroom by the new.

OLD TOWN
THE LANDS

THE OLD TOWN, it is pretended, is the chief characteristic, and, from a picturesque point of view, the liver-wing of Edinburgh. It is one of the most common forms of depreciation to throw cold water on the whole by adroit over-commendation of a part, since everything worth judging, whether it be a man, a work of art, or only a fine city, must be judged upon its merits as a whole. The Old Town depends for much of its effect on the new quarters that lie around it, on the sufficiency of its situation, and on the hills that back it up. If you were to set it somewhere else by itself, it would look remarkably like Stirling in a bolder and loftier edition. The point is to see this embellished Stirling planted in the midst of a large, active, and fantastic modern city; for there the two re-act in a picturesque sense, and the one is the making of the other.

The Old Town occupies a sloping ridge or tail of diluvial matter, protected, in some subsidence of the waters, by the Castle cliffs which fortify it to the west. On the one side of it and the other the new towns of the south and of the north occupy their lower, broader, and more gentle hill-tops. Thus, the quarter of the Castle overtops the whole city and keeps an open view to sea and land. It dominates for miles on every side; and people on the decks of ships, or ploughing in quiet country places over in Fife, can see the banner of the Castle battlements, and the smoke of the Old Town blowing abroad over the subjacent country. A city that is set upon a hill. It was, I suppose, from this distant aspect that she got her nickname *Auld Reekie*. Perhaps it was given her by people who had never crossed her doors: day after day, from their various rustic Pisgahs, they had seen the pile of buildings on the hill-top, and the long plume of smoke over the plain; so it appeared to them; so it had appeared to their fathers tilling the same field; and as that was all they knew of the place, it could be all expressed in these two words.

Indeed, even on a nearer view, the Old Town is properly smoked; and though it is well washed with rain all the year round, it has a grim and sooty aspect among its younger suburbs. It grew, under the law that regulates the growth of walled cities in precarious situations, not in extent, but in height and density. Public buildings were forced, wherever there was room for them, into the midst of thoroughfares; thoroughfares were diminished into lanes; houses sprang up story after story, neighbour mounting upon neighbour's shoulder, as in some Black Hole of Calcutta, until the population slept fourteen or fifteen deep in a vertical direction. The tallest of these *lands*, as they are locally termed, have long since been burnt out; but to this day it is not uncommon to see eight or ten windows at a flight; and the cliff of building which hangs imminent over Waverley Bridge would still put many natural precipices to shame. The cellars are already high above the gazer's head, planted on the steep hill-side; as for the garret, all the furniture may be in the pawnshop, but it commands a famous prospect to the Highland hills. The poor man may roost up there in the centre of Edinburgh, and yet have a peep of the green country from his window; he shall see the quarters of the well-to-do fathoms underneath, with their broad squares and gardens; he shall have nothing overhead but a few spires, the stone top-gallants of the city; and perhaps the wind may reach him with a rustic pureness, and bring a smack of the sea, or of flowering lilacs in the spring.

It is almost the correct literary sentiment to deplore the

Cowfeeder Row and Head of West Port

revolutionary improvements of Mr Chambers and his following. It is easy to be a conservator of the discomforts of others; indeed, it is only our good qualities we find it irksome to conserve.

Assuredly, in driving streets through the black labyrinth, a few curious old corners have been swept away, and some associations turned out of house and home. But what slices of sunlight, what breaths of clean air, have been let in! And what a picturesque world remains untouched! You go under dark arches, and down dark stairs and alleys. The way is so narrow that you can lay a hand on either wall; so steep that, in greasy winter weather, the pavement is almost as treacherous as ice. Washing dangles above washing from the windows; the houses bulge outwards upon flimsy brackets; you see a bit of sculpture in a dark corner; at the top of all, a gable and a few crowsteps are printed on the sky. Here, you come into a court where the children are at play and the grown people sit upon their doorsteps, and perhaps a church spire shows itself above the roofs. Here, in the narrowest of the entry, you find a great old mansion still erect, with some insignia of its former state — some scutcheon, some holy or courageous motto, on the lintel. The local antiquary points out where famous and well-born people had their lodging; and as you look up, out pops the head of a slatternly woman from the countess's window. The Bedouins camp within Pharaoh's palace walls, and the old war-ship is given over to the rats. We are already a far way from the days when powdered heads were plentiful in these alleys, with jolly, port-wine faces underneath. Even in the chief thoroughfares Irish washings flutter at the windows, and the pavements are encumbered with loiterers.

These loiterers are a true character of the scene. Some shrewd Scotch workmen may have paused on their way to a job, debating Church affairs and politics with their tools upon their arm. But the most part are a different order — skulking jail-birds; unkempt, bare-foot children; big-mouthed, robust women, in a sort of uniform of striped flannel petticoat and short tartan shawl: among these, a few supervising constables and a dismal sprinkling of mutineers and broken men from higher ranks in society, with some mark of better days upon them, like a brand. In a place no larger than Edinburgh, and where the traffic is mostly centered in five or six chief streets, the same face comes often under the notice of an idle stroller. In fact, from this point

Advocates Close
(Etching by W. E. Lockhart, R.S.A., from the original edition)

of view, Edinburgh is not so much a small city as the largest of small towns. It is scarce possible to avoid observing your neighbours; and I never yet heard of any one who tried. It has been my fortune, in this anonymous accidental way, to watch more than one of these downward travellers for some stages on the road to ruin. One man must have been upward of sixty before I first observed him, and he made then a decent, personable figure in broadcloth of the best. For three years he kept falling — grease coming and buttons going from the square-skirted coat, the face puffing and pimpling, the shoulders growing bowed, the hair falling scant and grey upon his head; and the last that I ever saw of him, he was standing at the mouth of an entry with several men in moleskin, three parts drunk, and his old black raiment daubed with mud. I fancy that I still can hear him laugh. There was something heart-breaking in this gradual declension at so advanced an age; you would have thought a man of sixty out of the reach of these calamities; you would have thought that he was niched by that time into a safe place in life, whence he could pass quietly and honourably into the grave.

One of the earliest marks of these *dégringolades*, is that the victim begins to disappear from the New Town thoroughfares, and takes to the High Street, like a wounded animal to the woods. And such an one is the type of the quarter. It also has fallen socially. A scutcheon over the door somewhat jars in

Advocates Close

sentiment where there is a washing at every window. The old man, when I saw him last, wore the coat in which he had played the gentleman three years before; and that was just what gave him so pre-eminent an air of wretchedness.

It is true that the over-population was at least as dense in the epoch of lords and ladies, and that now-a-days some customs which made Edinburgh notorious of yore have been fortunately pretermitted. But an aggregation of comfort is not distasteful like an aggregation of the reverse. Nobody cares how many lords and ladies, and divines and lawyers, may have been crowded into these houses in the past — perhaps the more the merrier. The glasses clink around the china punch-bowl, some one touches the virginals, there are peacocks' feathers on the chimney, and the tapers burn clear and pale in the red fire-light. That is not an ugly picture in itself, nor will it become ugly upon repetition. All the better if the like were going on in every second room; the *land* would only look the more inviting. Times are changed. In one house, perhaps, twoscore families herd together; and, perhaps, not one of them is wholly out of the reach of want. The great hotel is given over to discomfort from the foundation to the chimney-tops; everywhere a pinching, narrow habit, scanty meals, and an air of sluttishness and dirt. In the first room there is a birth, in another a death, in a third a sordid drinking-bout, and the detective and the Bible-reader cross upon the stairs. High words are audible from dwelling to dwelling, and children have a strange experience from the first: only a robust soul, you would think, could grow up in such conditions without hurt. And even if God tempers his dispensations to the young, and all the ill does not arise that our apprehensions may forecast, the sight of such a way of living is disquieting to people who are more happily circumstanced. Social inequality is nowhere more ostentatious than at Edinburgh. I have mentioned already how, to the stroller along Princes Street, the High Street callously exhibits its back garrets. It is true, there is a garden between. And although nothing could be more glaring by way of contrast, sometimes the opposition is more immediate; sometimes the thing lies in a nutshell, and there is not so much as a blade of grass between the rich and poor. To look over the South Bridge and see the Cowgate below full of crying hawkers, is to view one rank of society from another in the twinkling of an eye.

One night I went along the Cowgate after everyone was a-bed but the policeman, and stopped by hazard before a tall *land*. The moon touched upon its chimneys, and shone blankly on the upper windows; there was no light anywhere in the great bulk of building; but as I stood there it seemed to me that I could hear quite a body of quiet sounds from the interior; doubtless there were many clocks ticking, and people snoring on their backs. And thus, as I fancied, the dense life within made itself faintly audible in my ears, family after family contributing its quota to the general hum, and the whole pile beating in tune to its timepieces, like a great disordered heart. Perhaps it was little more than a fancy altogether, but it was strangely impressive at the time, and gave me an imaginative measure of the disproportion between the quantity of living flesh and the trifling walls that separated and contained it.

There was nothing fanciful, at least, but every circumstance of terror and reality; in the fall of the *land* in the High Street. The building had grown rotten to the core; the entry underneath had suddenly closed up so that the scavenger's barrow could not pass; cracks and reverberations sounded through the house at night; the inhabitants of the huge old human bee-hive discussed their peril when they encountered on the stair; some had even left their dwellings in a panic of fear, and returned to them again in a fit of economy or self-respect; when, in the black hours of a Sunday morning, the whole structure ran together with a hideous uproar and tumbled story upon story to the ground. The physical shock was felt far and near; and the moral shock travelled with the morning milkmaid into all the suburbs. The church-bells never sounded more dismally over Edinburgh than that grey forenoon. Death had made a brave harvest; and, like Samson, by pulling down one roof destroyed many a home. None who saw it can have forgotten the aspect of the gable: here it was plastered, there papered, according to the rooms; here the kettle still stood on the hob, high overhead; and there a cheap picture of the Queen

The Cowgate from South Bridge

was pasted over the chimney. So, by this disaster, you had a glimpse into the life of thirty families, all suddenly cut off from the revolving years. The *land* had fallen; and with the *land*, how much! Far in the country, people saw a gap in the city ranks, and the sun looked through between the chimneys in an unwonted place. And all over the world, in London, in Canada, in New Zealand, fancy what a multitude of people could exclaim with truth: 'The house that I was born in fell last night!'

Old Assembly Rooms, West Bow

THE
PARLIAMENT
CLOSE

TIME HAS wrought its changes most notably around the precinct of St Giles's Church. The church itself, if it were not for the spire, would be unrecognisable; the *Krames* are all gone, not a shop is left to shelter in its buttresses; and zealous magistrates and a misguided architect have shorn the design of manhood, and left it poor, naked, and pitifully pretentious. As St Giles's must have had in former days a rich and quaint appearance now forgotten, so the neighbourhood was bustling, sunless, and romantic. It was here that the town was most overbuilt; but the overbuilding has been all rooted out, and not only a free fairway left along the High Street with an open space on either side of the church, but a great porthole, knocked in the main line of the *lands*, gives an overlook to the north and the New Town.

There is a silly story of a subterranean passage between the Castle and Holyrood, and a bold Highland piper who volunteered to explore its windings. He made his entrance by the upper end, playing a strathspey; the curious footed it after him down the street, following his descent by the sound of the chanter from below; until all of a sudden, about the level of St Giles, the music came abruptly to an end, and the people in the street stood at fault with hands uplifted. Whether he was choked with gases, or perished in a quag, or was removed bodily by the Evil One,

· 37 ·

remains a point of doubt; but the piper has never again been seen or heard of from that day to this. Perhaps he wandered down into the land of Thomas the Rhymer, and some day, when it is least expected, may take a thought to revisit the sunlit upper world. That will be a strange moment for the cabmen on the stance beside St Giles's, when they hear the drone of his pipes reascending from the bowels of the earth below their horses' feet.

But it is not only pipers who have vanished, many a solid bulk of masonry has been likewise spirited into the air. Here, for example, is the shape of a heart let into the causeway. This was the site of the Tolbooth, the Heart of Midlothian, a place old in story and namefather to a noble book. The walls are now down in the dust; there is no more *squalor carceris* for merry debtors, no

St Giles' Cathedral

The Interior of St Giles' Cathedral

more cage for the old, acknowledged prison-breaker; but the sun and the wind play freely over the foundations of the jail. Nor is this the only memorial that the pavement keeps of former days. The ancient burying-ground of Edinburgh lay behind St Giles's Church, running downhill to the Cowgate and covering the site of the present Parliament House. It has disappeared as utterly as the prison or the Luckenbooths; and for those ignorant of its history, I know only one token that remains. In the Parliament Close, trodden daily underfoot by advocates, two letters and a

The Heart of Midlothian, and John Knox's grave

date mark the resting-place of the man who made Scotland over again in his own image, the indefatigable, undissuadable John Knox. He sleeps within call of the church that so often echoed to his preaching.

Hard by the reformer, a bandy-legged and garlanded Charles Second, made of lead, bestrides a tun-bellied charger. The King has his back turned, and, as you look, seems to be trotting clumsily away from such a dangerous neighbour. Often, for hours together, these two will be alone in the Close, for it lies out of the way of all but legal traffic. On one side the south wall of the church, on the other the arcades of the Parliament House, inclose this irregular bight of causeway and describe their shadows on it in the sun. At either end, from round St Giles's buttresses, you command a look into the High Street with its motley passengers; but the stream goes by, east and west, and leaves the Parliament Close to Charles the Second and the birds. Once in a while, a patient crowd may be seen loitering there all day, some eating fruit, some reading a newspaper; and to judge by their quiet demeanour, you would think they were waiting for a distribution of soup-tickets. The fact is far otherwise; within the **Justiciary Court** a man is upon trial for his life, and these are some of the curious for whom the gallery was found too narrow. Towards afternoon, if the prisoner is unpopular, there will be a round of hisses when he is brought forth. Once in a while, too, an advocate in wig and gown, hand upon mouth, full of pregnant nods, sweeps to and fro in the arcade listening to an agent; and at certain regular hours a whole tide of lawyers hurries across the space.

The Parliament Close has been the scene of marking incidents in Scottish history. Thus, when the Bishops were ejected from the Convention in 1688, 'all fourteen of them gathered together with pale faces and stood in a cloud in the Parliament Close:' poor episcopal personages who were done with fair weather for life! Some of the west-country Societarians standing by, who would have 'rejoiced more than in great sums' to be at their hanging, hustled them so rudely that they knocked their heads together. It was not magnanimous behaviour to dethroned enemies; but one, at least, of the Societarians had groaned in the *boots*, and they had all seen their dear friends upon the scaffold. Again, at the 'woeful Union,' it was here that people crowded to escort their favourite from the last of Scottish parliaments: people flushed with nationality, as Boswell would have said, ready for riotous acts, and fresh from throwing stones at the author of *Robinson Crusoe* as he looked out of window.

One of the pious in the seventeenth century, going to pass his *trials* (examinations as we now say) for the Scottish Bar, beheld the Parliament Close open and had a vision of the mouth of Hell. This, and small wonder, was the means of his conversion. Nor was the vision unsuitable to the locality; for after an hospital, what uglier piece is there in civilisation than a court of law? Hither come envy, malice and all uncharitableness to wrestle it out in public tourney; crimes, broken fortunes, severed households, the knave and his victim, gravitate to this low building with the arcade. To how many has not St Giles's bell told the first hour after ruin? I think I see them pause to count the strokes, and wander on again into the moving High Street, stunned and sick at heart.

A pair of swing doors gives admittance to a hall with a carved roof, hung with legal portraits, adorned with legal statuary, lighted by windows of painted glass, and warmed by three vast fires. This is the *Salle des pas perdus* of the Scottish Bar. Here, by a ferocious custom, idle youths must promenade from ten till two. From end to end, singly or in pairs or trios, the gowns and wigs go back and forward. Through a hum of talk and footfalls, the piping tones of a Macer announce a fresh cause and call upon

Statue of Sir Walter Scott in the Advocates' Library

the names of those concerned. Intelligent men have been walking here daily for ten or twenty years without a rag of business or a shilling of reward. In process of time, they may perhaps be made the Sheriff-Substitute and Fountain of Justice at Lerwick or Tobermory. There is nothing required, you would say, but a little patience and a taste for exercise and bad air. To breathe dust and bombazine, to feed the mind on cackling gossip, to hear three parts of a case and drink a glass of sherry, to long with indescribable longings for the hour when a man may slip out of his travesty and devote himself to golf for the rest of the afternoon, and to do this day by day and year after year, may seem so small a thing to the inexperienced! But those who have made the experiment are of a different way of thinking, and count it the most arduous form of idleness.

More swing doors open into pigeon-holes where Judges of the First Appeal sit singly, and halls of audience where the supreme Lords sit by three or four. Here, you may see Scott's place within the bar, where he wrote many a page of Waverley novels to the drone of judicial proceeding. You will hear a good deal of shrewdness, and, as their Lordships do not altogether disdain pleasantry, a fair proportion of dry fun. The broadest of broad Scotch is now banished from the bench; but the courts still retain a certain national flavour. We have a solemn enjoyable way of lingering on a case. We treat law as a fine art, and relish and digest a good distinction. There is no hurry: point after point must be rightly examined and reduced to principle; judge after judge must utter forth his *obiter dicta* to delighted brethren.

Besides the courts, there are installed under the same roof no less than three libraries; two of no mean order; confused and semi-subterranean, full of stairs and galleries; where you may see the most studious-looking wigs fishing out novels by lanthorn light, in the very place where the old Privy Council tortured Covenanters. As the Parliament House is built upon a slope, although it presents only one story to the north, it measures half-a-dozen at least upon the south; and range after range of vaults extend below the libraries. Few places are more characteristic of this hilly capital. You descend one stone stair after another, and wander, by the flicker of a match, in a labyrinth of stone cellars. Now, you pass below the Outer Hall and hear overhead, brisk but ghostly, the interminable pattering of legal feet. Now, you come upon a strong door with a wicket: on the other side are the cells of the police office and the trap-stair that gives admittance to the dock in the Justiciary Court. Many a foot that has gone up there lightly enough, has been dead-heavy in the descent. Many a man's life has been argued away from him during long hours in the court above. But just now that tragic stage is empty and silent like a church on a week-day, with the bench all sheeted up and nothing moving but the sunbeams on the wall. A little farther and you strike upon a room, not empty like the rest, but crowded with *productions* from bygone criminal cases: a grim lumber: lethal weapons, poisoned organs in a jar, a door with a shot hole through the panel, behind which a man fell dead. I cannot fancy why they should preserve them, unless it were against the Judgment Day. At length, as you continue to descend, you see a peep of yellow gaslight and hear a jostling, whispering noise ahead; next moment you turn a corner, and there, in a white-washed passage, is a machinery belt industriously turning on its wheels. You would think the engine had grown there of its own accord, like a cellar fungus, and would soon spin itself out and fill the vaults from end to end with its mysterious labours. In truth, it is only some gear of the steam ventilator; and you will find the engineers at hand, and may step out of their door into the sunlight. For all this while, you have not been descending towards the earth's centre, but only to the bottom of the hill and the foundations of the Parliament House; low down, to be sure, but still under the open heaven and in a field of grass. The daylight shines garishly on the back-windows of the Irish quarter; on broken shutters, wry gables, old palsied houses on the brink of ruin, a crumbling human pig-sty fit for human pigs. There are few signs of life, besides a scanty washing or a face at a window: the dwellers are abroad, but they will return at night and stagger to their pallets.

LEGENDS

*Tweeddale Court, scene
of the Begbie murder*

THE CHARACTER of a place is often most perfectly
expressed in its associations. An event strikes root and
grows into a legend, when it has happened amongst congenial
surroundings. Ugly actions, above all in ugly places, have the true
romantic quality, and become an undying property of their scene.
To a man like Scott, the different appearances of nature seemed
each to contain its own legend ready made, which it was his to call
forth: in such or such a place, only such or such events ought with
propriety to happen; and in this spirit he made the *Lady of the
Lake* for Ben Venue, the *Heart of Midlothian* for Edinburgh, and
the *Pirate*, so indifferently written but so romantically con-
ceived, for the desolate islands and roaring tideways of the
North. The common run of mankind have, from generation to
generation, an instinct almost as delicate as that of Scott; but
where he created new things, they only forget what is unsuitable
among the old; and by survival of the fittest, a body of tradition
becomes a work of art. So, in the low dens and high-flying garrets
of Edinburgh, people may go back upon dark passages in the
town's adventures, and chill their marrow with winter's tales
about the fire: tales that are singularly apposite and characteristic, not only of the old life, but of the very constitution of built
nature in that part, and singularly well qualified to add horror to
horror, when the wind pipes around the tall lands, and hoots

adown arched passages, **and the** far-spread wilderness of city **lamps** keeps quavering and flaring in the gusts.

Here, it is the tale of Begbie, the bank-porter, stricken to the **heart** at a blow and left in his blood within a step or two of the **crowded** High Street. There, people hush their voices over Burke **and Hare**; over drugs and violated graves, and the resurrection-men smothering their victims with their knees. Here, again, the fame of Deacon Brodie is kept piously fresh. A great man in his day was the Deacon; well seen in good society, crafty with his hands as a cabinet-maker, and one who could sing a song with taste. Many a citizen was proud to welcome the Deacon to supper, and dismissed him with regret at a timeous hour, who would have been vastly disconcerted had he known how soon, and in what guise, his visitor returned. Many stories are told of this redoubtable Edinburgh burglar, but the one I have in my mind most vividly gives the key of all the rest. A friend of

Brodie's Close
where the
Deacon lived,
with his keys
and dark lantern

Brodie's, nested some way towards heaven in one of these great *lands*, had told him of a projected visit to the country, and afterwards detained by some affairs, put it off and stayed the night in town. The good man had lain some time awake; it was far on in the small hours by the Tron bell; when suddenly there came a creak, a jar, a faint light. Softly he clambered out of bed and up to a false window which looked upon another room, and there, by the glimmer of a thieves' lantern, was his good friend the Deacon in a mask. It is characteristic of the town and the town's manners that this little episode should have been quietly tided over, and quite a good time elapsed before a great robbery, an escape, a Bow-Street runner, a cock-fight, an apprehension in a cupboard in Amsterdam, and a last step into the air off his own greatly-improved gallows drop, brought the career of Deacon William Brodie to an end. But still, by the mind's eye, he may be seen, a man harassed below a mountain of duplicity, slinking from a magistrate's supper-room to a thieves' ken, and pickeering among the closes by the flicker of a dark lamp.

Or where the Deacon is out of favour, perhaps some memory lingers of the great plagues, and of fatal houses still unsafe to enter with the memory of man. For in time of pestilence the discipline had been sharp and sudden, and what we now call 'stamping out contagion' was carried on with deadly rigour. The officials, in their gowns of grey, with a white St Andrew's cross on back and breast, and a white cloth carried before them on a staff, perambulated the city, adding the terror of man's justice to the fear of God's visitation. The dead they buried on the Borough Muir; the living who had concealed the sickness were drowned, if they were women, in the Quarry Holes, and if they were men, were hanged and gibbeted at their own doors; and wherever the evil had passed, furniture was destroyed and houses closed. And the most bogeyish part of the story is about such houses. Two generations back, they still stood dark and empty; people avoided them as they passed by; the boldest schoolboy only shouted through the keyhole and made off; for within, it was supposed, the plague lay ambushed like a basilisk, ready to flow forth and spread blain and pustule through the city. What a terrible next-door neighbour for superstitious citizens! A rat scampering within would send a shudder through the stoutest heart. Here, if you like, was a sanitary parable, addressed by our uncleanly forefathers to their own neglect.

And then we have Major Weir; for although even his house is now demolished, old Edinburgh cannot clear herself of his

Major Weir's House

unholy memory. He and his sister lived together in an odour of sour piety. She was a marvellous spinster; he had a rare gift of supplication, and was known among devout admirers by the name of Angelical Thomas. 'He was a tall, black man, and ordinarily looked down to the ground; a grim countenance, and a big nose. His garb was still a cloak, and somewhat dark, and he never went without his staff.' How it came about that Angelical Thomas was burned in company with his staff, and his sister in gentler manner hanged, and whether these two were simply religious maniacs of the more furious order, or had real as well as imaginary sins upon their old-world shoulders, are points happily beyond the reach of our intention. At least, it is suitable enough that out of this superstitious city some such example should have been put forth: the outcome and fine flower of dark and vehement religion. And at least the facts struck the public fancy and brought forth a remarkable family of myths. It would appear that the Major's staff went upon his errands, and even ran before him with a lantern on dark nights. Gigantic females, 'stentoriously laughing and gaping with tehees of laughter' at unseasonable hours of night and morning, haunted the purlieus of his abode. His house fell under such a load of infamy that no one dared to sleep in it, until municipal improvement levelled the structure with the ground. And my father has often been told in the nursery how the devil's coach, drawn by six coal-black horses with fiery eyes, would drive at night into the West Bow, and belated people might see the dead Major through the glasses.

Another legend is that of the two maiden sisters. A legend I am afraid it may be, in the most discreditable meaning of the term; or perhaps something worse — a mere yesterday's fiction. But it is a story of some vitality, and is worthy of a place in the Edinburgh kalendar. This pair inhabited a single room; from the facts, it must have been double-bedded; and it may have been of some dimensions: but when all is said, it was a single room. Here our two spinsters fell out — on some point of controversial divinity belike: but fell out so bitterly that there was never a word spoken between them, black or white, from that day forward. You would have thought they would separate: but no; whether from lack of means, or the Scottish fear of scandal, they continued to keep house together where they were. A chalk line drawn upon the floor separated their two domains; it bisected the doorway and the fireplace, so that each could go out and in, and do her cooking, without violating the territory of the other. So, for years, they coexisted in a hateful silence; their meals, their ablutions, their friendly visitors, exposed to an unfriendly scrutiny; and at night, in the dark watches, each could hear the breathing of her enemy. Never did four walls look down upon an uglier spectacle than these sisters rivalling in unsisterliness. Here is a canvas for Hawthorne to have turned into a cabinet picture — he had a Puritanic vein, which would have fitted him to treat this Puritanic horror; he could have shown them to us in their sicknesses and at their hideous twin devotions, thumbing a pair of great Bibles, or praying aloud for each other's penitence with marrowy emphasis; now each, with kilted petticoat, at her own corner of the fire on some tempestuous evening; now sitting each at her window, looking out upon the summer landscape sloping far below them towards the firth, and the field-paths where they had wandered hand in hand; or, as age and infirmity grew upon them and prolonged their toilettes, and their hands began to tremble and their heads to nod involuntarily, growing only the more steeled in enmity with years; until one fine day, at a word, a look, a visit, the approach of death, their hearts would melt and the chalk boundary be overstepped for ever.

Alas! to those who know the ecclesiastical history of the race — the most perverse and melancholy in man's annals — this will seem only a figure of much that is typical of Scotland and her high-seated capital above the Forth — a figure so grimly realistic that it may pass with strangers for a caricature. We are wonderful patient haters for conscience sake up here in the North. I spoke, in the first of these papers, of the Parliaments of the Established and Free Churches, and how they can hear each other singing psalms across the street. There is but a street between them in space, but a shadow between them in principle; and yet there they sit, enchanted, and in damnatory accents pray for each other's growth in grace. It would be well if there were no more than two; but the sects in Scotland form a large family of sisters, and the chalk lines are thickly drawn, and run through the midst of many private homes. Edinburgh is a city of churches, as though it were a place of pilgrimage. You will see four within a stone-cast at the head of the West Bow. Some are crowded to the doors; some are empty like monuments; and yet you will ever find new ones in the building. Hence that surprising clamour of church bells that suddenly breaks out upon the Sabbath morning, from Trinity and the sea-skirts to Morningside on the borders of the hills. I have heard the chimes of Oxford playing their symphony in a golden autumn morning, and beautiful it was to hear. But in Edinburgh all manner of loud bells join, or rather disjoin, in one swelling, brutal babblement of noise. Now one overtakes another, and now lags behind it; now five or six all strike on the pained tympanum of the same punctual instant of time, and make together a dismal chord of discord; and now, for a second, all seem to have conspired to hold their peace. Indeed, there are not many uproars in this world more dismal than that of the Sabbath bells in Edinburgh: a harsh ecclesiastical tocsin; the outcry of incongruous orthodoxies, calling on every separate conventicler to put up a protest, each in his own synagogue, against 'right-hand extremes and left-handed defections.' And surely there are few worse extremes than this extremity of zeal; and few more deplorable defections than this desloyalty to Christian love. Shakespeare wrote a comedy of *Much Ado about Nothing*. The Scottish nation made a fantastic tragedy on the same subject. And it is for the success of this remarkable piece that these bells are sounded every Sabbath morning on the hills above the Forth. How many of them might rest silent in the steeple, how many of these ugly churches might be demolished and turned once more into useful building material, if people who think almost exactly the same thoughts about religion would condescend to worship God under the same roof! But there are the chalk lines. And which is to pocket pride, and speak the foremost word?

GREYFRIARS

IT WAS Queen Mary who threw open the gardens of the Grey Friars: a new and semi-rural cemetery in those days, although it has grown an antiquity in its turn and been superseded by half-a-dozen others. The Friars must have had a pleasant time on summer evenings; for their gardens were situated to a wish, with the tall castle and the tallest of the castle crags in front. Even now, it is one of our famous Edinburgh points of view; and strangers are led thither to see, by yet another instance, how strangely the city lies upon her hills. The enclosure is of an irregular shape; the double church of Old and New Greyfriars stands on the level at the top; a few thorns are dotted here and there, and the ground falls by terrace and steep slope towards the north. The open shows many slabs and table-tombstones; and all round the margin, the place is girt by an array of aristocratic mausoleums appallingly adorned.

Setting aside the tombs of Roubilliac, which belong to the heroic order of graveyard art, we Scotch stand, to my fancy, highest among nations in the matter of grimly illustrating death. We seem to love for their own sake the emblems of time and the great change; and even around country churches you will find a wonderful exhibition of skulls, and crossbones, and nose-less angels, and trumpets pealing for the Judgment Day. Every mason was a pedestrian Holbein: he had a deep consciousness of death, and loved to put its terrors pithily before the churchyard loiterer; he was brimful of rough hints upon mortality, and any dead farmer was seized upon to be a text. The classical examples of this art are in Greyfriars. In their time, these were doubtless costly monuments and reckoned of a very elegant proportion by contemporaries ; and now, when the elegance is not so apparent, the significance remains. You may perhaps look with a smile on the profusion of Latin mottoes — some crawling endwise up the shaft of a pillar, some issuing on a scroll from angels' trumpets — on the emblematic horrors, the figures rising headless from the grave, and all the traditional ingenuities in which it pleased our fathers to set forth their sorrow for the dead and their sense of earthly mutability. But it is not a hearty sort of mirth. Each ornament may have been executed by the merriest apprentice, whistling as he plied the mallet ; but the original meaning of each, and the combined effect of so many of them in this quiet enclosure, is serious to the point of melancholy.

Round a great part of the circuit, houses of a low class present their backs to the churchyard. Only a few inches separate the living from the dead. Here, a window is partly blocked up by the pediment of a tomb ; there, where the street falls far below the level of the graves, a chimney has been trained up the back of a monument, and a red pot looks vulgarly over from behind. A damp smell of the graveyard finds its way into houses where workmen sit at meat. Domestic life on a small scale goes forward visibly at the windows. The very solitude and stillness of the enclosure, which lies apart from the town's traffic, serves to accentuate the contrast. As you walk upon the graves, you see children scattering crumbs to feed the sparrows ; you hear people singing or washing dishes, or the sound of tears and castigation; the linen on a clothespole flaps against funereal sculpture ; or perhaps the cat slips over the lintel and descends on a memorial urn. And as there is nothing else astir, these incongruous sights and noises take hold on the attention and exaggerate the sadness of the place.

Greyfriars is continually overrun by cats. I have seen, one winter afternoon, as many as thirteen of them seated on the grass beside old Milne, the Master Builder, all sleek and fat and complacently blinking, as if they had fed upon strange meats. Old Milne was chaunting with the saints, as we may hope, and cared

little for the company about his grave ; but I confess the spectacle had an ugly side for me ; and I was glad to step forward and raise my eyes to where the Castle and the roofs of the Old Town, and the spire of the Assembly Hall, stood deployed against the sky with the colourless precision of engraving. An open outlook is to be desired from a churchyard, and a sight of the sky and some of the world's beauty relieves a mind from morbid thoughts.

I shall never forget one visit. It was a grey, dropping day ; the grass was strung with raindrops ; and the people in the houses kept hanging out their shirts and petticoats and angrily taking them in again, as the weather turned from wet to fair and back again. A gravedigger, and a friend of his, a gardener from the country, accompanied me into one after another of the cells and little courtyards in which it gratified the wealthy of old days to enclose their bones from neighbourhood. In one, under a sort of shrine, we found a forlorn human effigy, very realistically executed down to the detail of his ribbed stockings, and holding in his hand a ticket with the date of his demise. He looked most pitiful and ridiculous, shut up by himself in his aristocratic precinct, like a bad old boy or an inferior forgotten deity under a new dispensation ; the burdocks grew familiarly about his feet, the rain dripped all round him ; and the world maintained the most entire indifference as to who he was or whither he had gone. In another, a vaulted tomb, handsome externally but horrible inside with damp and cobwebs, there were three mounds of black earth and an uncovered thigh bone. This was the place of interment, it appeared, of a family with whom the gardener had been long in service. He was among old acquaintances. 'This'll be Miss Marg'et's,' said he, giving the bone a friendly kick. 'The auld ————!' I have always an uncomfortable feeling in a graveyard, at sight of so many tombs to perpetuate memories best forgotten; but I never had the impression so strongly as that day. People had been at some expense in both these cases: to provoke a melancholy feeling of derision in the one, and an an insulting epithet in the other. The proper inscription for the most part of mankind, I began to think, is the cynical jeer, *cras tibi.* That, if anything, will stop the mouth of a carper ; since it both admits the worst and carries the war triumphantly into the enemy's camp.

Greyfriars is a place of many associations. There was one window in a house at the lower end, now demolished, which was pointed out to me by the gravedigger as a spot of legendary interest. Burke, the resurrection man, infamous for so many murders at five shillings a-head, used to sit thereat, with pipe and nightcap, to watch burials going forward on the green. In a tomb higher up, which must then have been but newly finished, John Knox, according to the same formant, had taken refuge in a turmoil of the Reformation. Behind the church is the haunted mausoleum of Sir George Mackenzie: Bloody Mackenzie, Lord Advocate in the Covenanting troubles and author of some pleasing sentiments on toleration. Here, in the last century, an old Heriot's Hospital boy once harboured from the pursuit of the police. The Hospital is next door to Greyfriars — a courtly building among lawns, where, on Founder's Day, you may see a multitude of children playing Kiss-in-the-Ring and Round the Mulberry-bush. Thus, when the fugitive had managed to conceal

himself in the tomb, his old schoolmates had a hundred opport-
unities to bring him food ; and there he lay in safety till a ship
was found to smuggle him abroad. But his must have been indeed
a heart of brass, to lie all day and night alone with the dead
persecutor ; and other lads were far from emulating him in
courage. When a man's soul is certainly in hell, his body will
scarce lie quiet in a tomb however costly ; some time or other the
door must open, and the reprobate come forth in the abhorred
garments of the grave. It was thought a high piece of prowess to
knock at the Lord Advocate's mausoleum and challenge him to
appear. 'Bluidy Mackingie, come oot if ye dar'!' sang the
foolhardy urchins. But Sir George had other affairs on hand ; and
the author of an essay on toleration continues to sleep peace-
fully among the many whom he so intolerantly helped to slay.

For this *infelix campus*, as it is dubbed in one of its own
inscriptions — an inscription over which Dr Johnson passed a
critical eye — is in many ways sacred to the memory of the men

whom Mackenzie persecuted. It was here, on the flat tomb-stones, that the Covenant was signed by an enthusiastic people. In the long arm of the churchyard that extends to Lauriston, the prisoners from Bothwell Bridge — fed on bread and water and guarded, life for life, by vigilant marksmen — lay five months looking for the scaffold or the plantations. And while the good work was going forward in the Grass Market, idlers in Greyfriars might have heard the throb of the military drums that drowned the voices of the martyrs. Nor is this all: for down in the corner farthest from Sir George, there stands a monument dedicated, in uncouth Covenanting verse, to all who lost their lives in that contention. There is no moorsman shot in a snow shower beside Irongray or Co'monell; there is not one of the two hundred who were drowned off the Orkneys; nor so much as a poor, over-driven, Covenanting slave in the American plantations; but can lay claim to a share in that memorial and, if such things interest just men among the shades, can boast he has a monument on earth as well as Julius Cæsar or the Pharaohs. Where they may all lie, I know not. Far-scattered bones, indeed! But if the reader cares to learn how some of them — or some part of some of them — found their way at length to such honourable sepulchre, let him listen to the words of one who was their comrade in life and their apologist when they were dead. Some of the insane controversial matter I omit, as well as some digressions, but leave the rest in Patrick Walker's language and orthography:—

'The never to be forgotten Mr *James Renwick* told me, that he was Witness to their Public Murder of the *Gallowlee*, between *Leith* and *Edinburgh*, when he saw the Hangman hash and hag off all their Five Heads, with *Patrick Foreman's* Right Hand: Their Bodies were all buried at the Gallows Foot; their Heads, with *Patrick's* Hand, were brought and put upon five Pikes on the *Pleasaunce-Port* . . . Mr *Renwick* told me also that it was the first public Action that his Hand was at, to conveen Friends, and lift their murthered Bodies, and carried them to the West Churchyard ●f *Edinburgh*,' — not Greyfriars, this time, — 'and buried them there. Then they came about the City . . . and took down these Five Heads and that Hand; and Day being come, they went quickly up the *Pleasaunce*; and when they came to *Lauristoun* Yards, upon the South-side of the City, they durst not venture, being so light, to go and bury their Heads with their Bodies, which they designed; it being present Death, if any of them had been found. *Alexander*

Tweedie, a friend, being with them, who at that Time was Gardner in these Yards, concluded to bury them in his Yard, being in a Box (wrapped in Linen), where they lay 45 Years except 3 Days, being executed upon the 10th of *October* 1681, and found the 7th Day of *October* 1726. That Piece of Ground lay for some Years unlaboured; and trenching it, the Gardner found them, which affrighted him; the Box was consumed. Mr *Schaw*, the Owner of these Yards, caused lift them, and lay them upon a Table in his Summer-house: Mr *Schaw's* mother was so kind, as to cut out a Linen-cloth, and cover them. They lay Twelve Days there, where all had Access to see them. Alexander Tweedie, the foresaid Gardner, said, when dying, There was a Treasure hid in his Yard, but neither Gold nor Silver. *Daniel Tweedie*, his Son, came along with me to that Yard, and told me that his Father planted a white Rose-bush above them, and farther down the Yard a red Rose-bush, which were more fruitful than any other Bush in the Yard … Many came' — to see the heads — 'out of Curiosity; yet I rejoiced to see so many concerned grave Men and Women favouring the Dust of Martyrs. There were Six of us concluded to bury them upon the Nineteenth Day of *October* 1726, and every One of us to acquaint Friends of the Day and Hour, being *Wednesday*, the Day of the Week on which most of them were executed, and at 4 of the Clock at Night, being the Hour that most of them went to their resting Graves. We caused make a compleat Coffin'for them in Black, with four Yards of fine Linen, the way that our Martyrs Corps were managed … Accordingly we kept the foresaid Day and Hour, and doubled the Linen, and laid the Half of it below them, their nether Jaws being parted from their Heads; but being young Men, their Teeth remained. All were Witness to the Holes in each of their Heads, which the Hangman broke with his Hammer; and according to the Bigness of their Sculls, we laid the Jaws to them, and drew the other Half of the Linen above them, and stufft the Coffin with Shavings. Some prest hard to go thorow the chief Parts of the City as was done at the Revolution; but this we refused, considering that it looked airy and frothy, to make such Show of them, and inconsistent with the solid serious Observing of such an affecting, surprizing unheard-of Dispensation: But took the ordinary Way of other Burials from that Place, to wit, we went east the Back of the Wall, and in at *Bristo-Port*, and down the Way to the Head of the *Cowgate*, and turned up to the Church-yard, where they were interred closs to the Martyrs Tomb, with the greatest Multitude of People Old and Young, Men and Women, Ministers and others, that ever I saw together.'

And so there they were at last, in 'their resting graves.' So long as men do their duty, even if it be greatly in a misapprehension, they will be leading pattern lives; and whether or not they come to lie beside a martyrs' monument, we may be sure they will find a safe haven somewhere in the providence of God. It is not well to think of death, unless we temper the thought with that of heroes who despised it. Upon what ground, is of small account; if it be only the bishop who was burned for his faith in the antipodes, his memory lightens the heart and makes us walk undisturbed among graves. And so the martyrs' monument is a wholesome, heartsome spot in the field of the dead; and as we look upon it, a brave influence comes to us from the land of those who have won their discharge and, in another phrase of Patrick Walker's, got 'cleanly off the stage'.

Mackenzie's Tomb

NEW TOWN
TOWN AND COUNTRY

IT IS as much a matter of course to decry the New Town
as to exalt the Old; and the most celebrated authorities have
picked out this quarter as the very emblem of what is condemn-
able in architecture. Much may be said, much indeed has been
said, upon the text; but to the unsophisticated, who call
anything pleasing if it only pleases them, the New Town of
Edinburgh seems, in itself, not only gay and airy, but highly
picturesque. An old skipper, invincibly ignorant of all theories of
the sublime and beautiful, once propounded as his most radiant
notion for Paradise: 'The new town of Edinburgh, with the wind
the matter of a point free.' He has now gone to that sphere where
all good tars are promised pleasant weather in the song, and
perhaps his thoughts fly somewhat higher. But there are bright
and temperate days — with soft air coming from the inland hills,
military music sounding bravely from the hollow of the gardens,
the flags all waving on the palaces of Princes Street — when I have
seen the town through a sort of glory, and shaken hands in
sentiment with the old sailor. And indeed, for a man who has
been much tumbled round Orcadian skerries, what scene could
be more agreeable to witness? On such a day, the valley wears a
surprising air of festival. It seems (I do not know how else to put
my meaning) as if it were a trifle too good to be true. It is what
Paris ought to be. It has the scenic quality that would best set off
a life of unthinking, open-air diversion. It was meant by nature
for the realisation of the society of comic operas. And you can
imagine, if the climate were but towardly, how all the world and

his wife would flock into these gardens in the cool of the evening, to hear cheerful music, to sip pleasant drinks, to see the moon rise from behind Arthur's Seat and shine upon the spires and monuments and the green tree-tops in the valley. Alas! and the next morning the rain is splashing on the window, and the passengers flee along Princes Street before the galloping squalls.

It cannot be denied that the original design was faulty and short-sighted, and did not fully profit by the capabilities of the situation. The architect was essentially a town bird, and he laid out the modern city with a view to street scenery, and to street scenery alone. The country did not enter into his plan; he had never lifted his eyes to the hills. If he had so chosen, every street upon the northern slope might have been a noble terrace and commanded an extensive and beautiful view. But the space has been too closely built; many of the houses front the wrong way, intent, like the Man with the Muck-Rake, on what is not worth observation, and standing discourteously back-foremost in the ranks; and in a word, it is too often only from attic windows, or here and there at a crossing, that you can get a look beyond the city upon its diversified surroundings. But perhaps it is all the more· surprising, to come suddenly on a corner, and see a perspective of a mile or more of falling street, and beyond that woods and villas, and a blue arm of sea, and the hills upon the farther side.

Fergusson, our Edinburgh poet, Burns's model, once saw a butterfly at the Town Cross; and the sight inspired him with a

New Town and the Forth

Leith Street

worthless little ode. This painted country man, the dandy of the rose garden, looked far abroad in such a humming neighbourhood; and you can fancy what moral considerations a youthful poet would supply. But the incident, in a fanciful sort of way, is characteristic of the place. Into no other city does the sight of the country enter so far; if you do not meet a butterfly, you shall certainly catch a glimpse of far-away trees upon your walk; and the place is full of theatre tricks in the way of scenery. You peep under an arch, you descend stairs that look as if they would land you in a cellar, you turn to the back-window of a grimy tenement in a lane:— and behold! you are face-to-face with distant and bright prospects. You turn a corner, and there is the sun going down into the Highland hills. You look down an alley, and see ships tacking for the Baltic.

For the country people to see Edinburgh or her hill-tops, is one thing; it is another for a citizen, from the thick of his affairs, to overlook the country. It should be a genial and ameliorating influence in life; it should prompt good thoughts and remind him of Nature's unconcern: that he can watch from day to day, as he trots officeward, how the Spring green brightens in the wood or the field grows black under a moving ploughshare. I have been tempted, in this connexion, to deplore the slender faculties of the human race, with its penny-whistle of a voice, its dull ears, and its narrow range of sight. If you could see as people are to see in heaven, if you had eyes such as you can fancy for a superior race, if you could take clear note of the objects of vision, not only a few yards, but a few miles from where you stand: — think how agreeably your sight would be entertained, how pleasantly your thoughts would be diversified, as you walked the Edinburgh streets! For you might pause, in some business perplexity, in the midst of the city traffic, and perhaps catch the eye of a shepherd as he sat down to breathe upon a heathery shoulder of the Pentlands; or perhaps some urchin, clambering in a country elm, would put aside the leaves and show you his flushed and rustic visage; or a fisher racing seawards, with the tiller under his elbow, and the sail sounding in the wind, would fling you a salutation from between Anst'er and the May.

To be old is not the same thing as to be picturesque; **nor because the Old Town bears a strange physiognomy, does it at all follow** that the New Town shall look commonplace. Indeed, **apart** from antique houses, it is curious how much description **would** apply commonly to either. The same sudden accidents of ground, a similar dominating site above the plain, and the same superposition of one rank of society over another, are to be observed in both. Thus, the broad and comely approach to Prince's Street from the east, lined with hotels and public offices, makes a leap over the gorge of the Low Calton; if you cast a glance over the parapet, you look direct into that sunless and disreputable confluent of Leith Street; and the same tall houses open upon both thoroughfares. This is only the New Town passing overhead above its own cellars; walking, so to speak, over its own children, as is the way of cities and the human race. But at the Dean Bridge, you may behold a spectacle of a more novel

In the Village of Dean

order. The river runs at the bottom of a deep valley, among rocks and between gardens; the crest of either bank is occupied by some of the most commodious streets and crescents in the modern city; and a handsome bridge unites the two summits. Over this, every afternoon, private carriages go spinning by, and ladies with card-cases pass to and fro about the duties of society. And yet down below, you may still see, with its mills and foaming weir, the little rural village of Dean. Modern improvement has gone overhead on its high-level viaduct; and the extended city has cleanly overleapt, and left unaltered, what was once the summer retreat of its comfortable citizens. Every town embraces hamlets in its growth; Edinburgh herself has embraced a good few; but it is strange to see one still surviving — and to see it some hundreds of feet below your path. Is it Torre del Greco that is built above buried Herculaneum? Herculaneum was dead at least; but the sun still shines upon the roofs of Dean; the smoke still rises thriftily from its chimneys; the dusty miller comes to his door, looks at the gurgling water, hearkens to the turning wheel and the birds about the shed, and perhaps whistles an air of his own to enrich the symphony — for all the world as if Edinburgh were still the old Edinburgh on the Castle Hill, and Dean were still the quietest of hamlets buried a mile or so in the green country.

It is not so long ago since magisterial David Hume lent the authority of his example to the exodus from the Old Town, and took up his new abode in a street which is still (so oddly may a jest become perpetuated) known as Saint David Street. Nor is the town so large but a holiday schoolboy may harry a bird's nest within half a mile of his own door. There are places that still smell of the plough in memory's nostrils. Here, one had heard a blackbird on a hawthorn; there, another was taken on summer evenings to eat strawberries and cream; and you have seen a waving wheatfield on the site of your present residence. The memories of an Edinburgh boy are but partly memories of the town. I look back with delight on many an escalade of garden walls; many a ramble among lilacs full of piping birds; many an exploration in obscure quarters that were neither town nor country; and I think that both for my companions and myself, there was a special interest, a point of romance, and a sentiment as of foreign travel, when we hit in our excursions on the butt-end of some former hamlet, and found a few rustic cottages embedded among streets and squares. The tunnel to the Scotland Street Station, the sight of the trains shooting out of its dark maw with the two guards upon the brake, the thought of its length and the many ponderous edifices and open thoroughfares above, were certainly things of paramount impressiveness to a young mind. It was a subterranean passage, although of a larger bore than we were accustomed to in Ainsworth's novels; and these two words, 'subterranean passage', were in themselves an irresistible attraction, and seemed to bring us nearer in spirit to the heroes we loved and the black rascals we secretly aspired to imitate. To scale the Castle Rock from West Prince's Street Gardens, and lay a triumphal hand against the rampart itself, was

to taste a high order of romantic pleasure. And there are other sights and exploits which crowd back upon my mind under a very strong illumination of remembered pleasure. But the effect of not one of them all will compare with the discoverer's joy, and the sense of old Time and his slow changes of the face of this earth, with which I explored such corners as Cannonmills or Water

Lane, or the nugget of cottages at Broughton Market. They were more rural than the open country, and gave a greater impression of antiquity than the oldest *land* upon the High Street. They too, like Fergusson's butterfly had a quaint air of having wandered far from their own place; they looked abashed and homely, with their gables and their creeping plants, their outside stairs and running mill-streams; there were corners that smelt like the end of the country garden where I spent my Aprils; and the people stood to gossip at their doors, as they might have done in Colinton or Cramond.

In a great measure we may, and shall, eradicate this haunting flavour of the country. The last elm is dead in Elm Row; and the villas and the workmen's quarters spread apace on all the borders of the city. We can cut down the trees; we can bury the grass under dead paving-stones; we can drive brisk streets through all our sleepy quarters; and we may forget the stories and the play-grounds of our boyhood. But we have some possessions that not even the infuriate zeal of builders can utterly abolish or destroy. Nothing can abolish the hills, unless it be a cataclysm of nature which shall subvert Edinburgh Castle itself and lay all her florid structures in the dust. And as long as we have the hills and the Firth, we have a famous heritage to leave our children. Our windows, at no expense to us, are most artfully stained to represent a landscape. And when the Spring comes round, and the hawthorn begins to flower, and the meadows to smell of young grass, and even in the thickest of our streets, the country hill-tops find out a young man's eyes, and set his heart beating for travel and pure air.

*View from
Dean Bridge*

THE VILLA
QUARTERS

M R RUSKIN'S denunciation of the New Town in Edinburgh includes, as I have heard it repeated, nearly all the
stone and lime we have to show. Many however find a grand air
and something settled and imposing in the better parts; and upon
many, as I have said, the confusion of styles induces an agreeable
stimulation of the mind. But upon the subject of our recent villa
architecture, I am frankly ready to mingle my tears with Mr
Ruskin's, and it is a subject which makes one envious of his large
declamatory and controversial eloquence.

Day by day, one new villa, one new object of offence, is added
to another; all around Newington and Morningside, the dis-
mallest structures keep springing up like mushrooms; the
pleasant hills are loaded with them, each impudently squatted in
its garden, each roofed and carrying chimneys like a house. And
yet a glance of an eye discovers their true character. They are not
houses; for they were not designed with a view to human
habitation, and the internal arrangements are, as they tell
me, fantastically unsuited to the needs of man. They are not
buildings; for you can scarcely say a thing is built where every
measurement is in clamant disproportion with its neighbour.
They belong to no style of art, only to a form of business much
to be regretted.

Why should it be cheaper to erect a structure where the size of
the windows bears no rational relation to the size of the front? Is
there any profit in a misplaced chimney-stalk? Does a hard-

working, greedy builder gain more on a monstrosity than on a decent cottage of equal plainness? Frankly, we should say, No. Bricks may be omitted, and green timber employed, in the construction of even a very elegant design; and there is no reason why a chimney should be made to vent, because it is so situated as to look comely from without. On the other hand, there is a noble way of being ugly: a high-aspiring fiasco like the fall of Lucifer. There are daring and gaudy buildings that manage to be offensive, without being contemptible; and we know that 'fools rush in where angels fear to tread.' But to aim at making a common-place villa, and to make it insufferably ugly in each particular ; to attempt the homeliest achievement and to attain the bottom of derided failure; not to have any theory but profit and yet, at an equal expense, to outstrip all competitors in the art of conceiving and rendering permanent deformity; and to do all this in what is, by nature, one of the most agreeable neighbour-hoods in Britain: — what are we to say, but that this also is a distinction, hard to earn although not greatly worshipful?

Indifferent buildings give pain to the sensitive; but these things offend the plainest taste. It is a danger which threatens the amenity of the town; and as this eruption keeps spreading on our borders, we have ever the farther to walk among unpleasant sights, before we gain the country air. If the population of Edinburgh were a living, autonomous body, it would arise like one man and make night hideous with arson; the builders and their accomplices would be driven to work, like the Jews of yore, with the trowel in one hand and the defensive cutlass in the other; and as soon as one of these masonic wonders had been consummated, right-minded iconoclasts should fall thereon and make an end of it at once.

Possibly these words may meet the eye of a builder or two. It is no use asking them to employ an architect; for that would be to touch them in a delicate quarter, and its use would largely depend on what architect they were minded to call in. But let them get any architect in the world to point out any reasonably well-proportioned villa, not his own design; and let them reproduce that model to satiety.

THE
CALTON
HILL

THE EAST of new Edinburgh is guarded by a craggy hill, of no great elevation, which the town embraces. The old London road runs on one side of it; while the New Approach, leaving it on the other hand, completes the circuit. You mount by stairs in a cutting of the rock to find yourself in a field of monuments. Dugald Stewart has the honours of situation and architecture; Burns is memorialised lower down upon a spur; Lord Nelson, as befits a sailor, gives his name to the topgallant of the Calton Hill. This latter erection has been differently and yet, in both cases, aptly compared to a telescope and a butterchurn; comparisons apart, it ranks among the vilest of men's handiworks. But the chief feature is an unfinished range of columns, 'the Modern Ruin' as it has been called, an imposing object from far and near, and giving Edinburgh, even from the sea, that false air of a Modern Athens which has earned for her so many slighting speeches. It was meant to be a National Monument; and its present state is a very suitable monument to certain national characteristics. The old Observatory — a quaint brown building on the edge of the steep — and the new Observatory — a classical edifice with a dome — occupy the central portion of the summit. All these are scattered on a green turf, browsed over by some sheep.

The scene suggests reflections on fame and on man's injustice to the dead. You see Dugald Stewart rather more handsomely commemorated than Burns. Immediately below, in the Canongate churchyard, lies Robert Fergusson, Burns's master in his art, who died insane while yet a stripling; and if Dugald Stewart has been somewhat too boisterously acclaimed, the Edinburgh poet, on the other hand, is most unrighteously forgotten. The votaries of Burns, a crew too common in all ranks in Scotland and more remarkable for number than discretion, eagerly suppress all mention of the lad who handed on to him the poetic impulse and, up to the time when he grew famous, continued to influence him in his manner and the choice of subjects. Burns himself not only acknowledged his debt in a fragment of autobiography, but erected a tomb over the grave in Canongate churchyard. This was worthy of an artist, but it was done in vain; and although I think I have read nearly all the biographies of Burns, I cannot remember one in which the modesty of nature was not violated, or where Fergusson was not sacrificed to the credit of his follower's originality. There is a kind of gaping admiration that would fain roll Shakespeare and Bacon into one, to have a bigger thing to gape at; and a class of men who cannot edit one author without disparaging all others. They are indeed mistaken if they think to please the great originals; and whoever puts Fergusson right with fame, cannot do better than dedicate his labours to Burns, who will be the best delighted of the dead.

Of all places for a view, this Calton Hill is perhaps the best; since you can see the Castle, which you lose from the Castle, and Arthur's Seat, which you cannot see from Arthur's Seat. It is the place to stroll on one of those days of sunshine and east wind which are so common in our more than temperate summer. The breeze comes off the sea, with a little of the sea freshness, and that touch of chill, peculiar to the quarter, which is delightful to certain very ruddy organizations and greatly the reverse to the majority of mankind. It brings with it a faint floating haze, a cunning decolourizer, although not thick enough to obscure outlines near at hand. But the haze lies more thickly to windward at the far end of Musselburgh Bay; and over the Links of Aberlady and Berwick Law and the hump of the Bass Rock it assumes the aspect of a bank of thin sea fog.

Immediately underneath upon the south, you command the yards of the High School and the towers and courts of the new

*Fergusson's
Tomb*

*Queen Mary's
Bathhouse*

Jail — a large place, castellated to the extent of folly, standing by itself on the edge of a steep cliff, and often joyfully hailed by tourists as the Castle. In the one, you may perhaps see female prisoners taking exercise like a string of nuns; in the other, schoolboys running at play and their shadows keeping step with them. From the bottom of the valley, a gigantic chimney rises almost to the level of the eye, a taller and a shapelier edifice than Nelson's Monument. Look a little farther, and there is Holyrood Palace, with its gothic frontal and ruined abbey, and the red sentry pacing smartly to and fro before the door like a mechanical figure in a panorama. By way of an outpost, you can single out the little peak-roofed lodge, over which Rizzio's murderers made their escape and where Queen Mary herself, according to gossip, bathed in white wine to entertain her loveliness. Behind and overhead, lie the Queen's Park, from Muschat's Cairn to Dumbiedykes, St Margaret's Loch, and the long wall of Salisbury Crags; and thence, by knoll and rocky bulwark and precipitous

Doorway to Holyrood Chapel

Arthur's Seat

slope, the eye rises to the top of Arthur's Seat, a hill for magnitude, a mountain in virtue of its bold design. This upon your left. Upon the right, the roofs and spires of the Old Town climb one above another to where the citadel prints its broad bulk and jagged crown of bastions on the western sky. — Perhaps it is now one in the afternoon; and at the same instant of time, a ball rises to the summit of Nelson's flagstaff close at hand, and, far away, a puff of smoke followed by a report bursts from the half-moon battery at the Castle. This is the time-gun by which people set their watches, as far as the sea coast or in hill farms upon the Pentlands. — To complete the view, the eye enfilades Prince's Street, black with traffic, and has a broad look over the valley between the Old Town and the New: here, full of railway trains and stepped over by the high North Bridge upon its many columns, and there, green with trees and gardens.

On the north, the Calton Hill is neither so abrupt in itself nor has it so exceptional an outlook; and yet even here it commands a striking prospect. A gully separates it from the New Town. This is Greenside, where witches were burned and tournaments held in former days. Down that almost precipitous bank, Bothwell launched his horse, and so first, as they say, attracted the bright eyes of Mary. It is now tesselated with sheets and blankets out to dry, and the sound of people beating carpets is rarely absent. Beyond all this, the suburbs run out to Leith; Leith camps on the seaside with her forest of masts; Leith roads are full of ships at anchor; the sun picks out the white pharos upon Inchkeith Island; the Firth extends on either hand from the Ferry to the May; the towns of Fifeshire sit, each in its bank of blowing smoke, along the opposite coast; and the hills enclose the view, upon the open sea. There lies the road to Norway: a dear road for Sir Patrick Spens and his Scots Lords; and yonder smoke on the hither side of Largo Law is Aberdour, from whence they sailed to seek a queen for Scotland.

> O lang, lang, may the ladies sit,
>   Wi' their fans into their hand,
> Or ere they see Sir Patrick Spens
>   Come sailing to the land!

The sight of the sea, even from a city, will bring thoughts of storm and sea disaster. The sailors' wives of Leith and the fisherwomen of Cockenzie, not sitting languorously with fans, but crowding to the tail of the harbour with a shawl about their ears, may still look vainly for brave Scotsmen who will return no more or boats that have gone on their last fishing. Since Sir Patrick sailed from Aberdour, what a multitude have gone down in the North Sea! Yonder is Auldhame, where the London smack went ashore and wreckers cut the rings from ladies' fingers; and a few miles round Fife Ness is the fatal Inchcape, now a star of guidance; and the lee shore to the east of the Inchcape, is that Forfarshire coast where Mucklebackit sorrowed for his son.

These are the main features of the scene roughly sketched. How they are all tilted by the inclination of the ground, how each stands out in delicate relief against the rest, what manifold detail, and play of sun and shadow, animate and accentuate the picture, is a matter for a person on the spot, and turning swiftly on his heels, to grasp and bind together in one comprehensive look. It is the character of such a prospect, to be full of change and of things moving. The multiplicity embarrasses the eye; and the mind, among so much, suffers itself to grow absorbed with single points. You remark a tree in a hedgerow, or follow a cart along a country road. You turn to the city, and see children, dwarfed by distance into pigmies, at play about suburban doorsteps; you have a glimpse upon a thoroughfare where people are densely moving; you note ridge after ridge of chimney-stacks running downhill one behind another, and church spires rising bravely from the sea of roofs, At one of the innumerable windows, you watch a figure moving; on one of the multitude of roofs, you watch clambering chimney-sweeps. The wind takes a run and scatters the smoke; bells are heard, far and near, faint and loud, to tell the hour; or perhaps a bird goes dipping evenly over the housetops, like a gull across the waves. And here you are in the meantime, on this pastoral hillside, among nibbling sheep and looked upon by monumental buildings.

Return thither on some clear, dark, moonless night, with a ring of frost in the air, and only a star or two set sparsely in the vault of heaven; and you will find a sight as stimulating as the hoariest summit of the Alps. The solitude seems perfect; the patient astronomer, flat on his back under the Observatory dome and spying heaven's secrets, is your only neighbour; and yet from all round you there come up the dull hum of the city, the tramp of countless people marching out of time, the rattle of carriages and the continuous, keen jingle of the tramway bells. An hour or so before, the gas was turned on; lamp-lighters scoured the city; in every house, from kitchen to attic, the windows kindled and gleamed forth into the dusk. And so now, although the town lies blue and darkling on her hills, innumerable spots of the bright element shine far and near along the pavements and upon the high facades. Moving lights of the railway pass and re-pass below the stationary lights upon the bridge. Lights burn in the Jail. Lights burn high up in the tall *lands* and on the Castle turrets, they burn low down in Greenside or along the Park. They run out one beyond the other into the dark country. They walk in a procession down to Leith, and shine singly far along Leith Pier. Thus, the plan of the city and her suburbs is mapped out upon the ground of blackness, as when a child pricks a drawing full of pinholes and exposes it before a candle; not the darkest night of winter can conceal her high station and fanciful design; every evening in the year she proceeds to illuminate herself in honour of her own beauty; and as if to complete the scheme — or rather as if some prodigal Pharoah were beginning to extend it to the adjacent sea and country — half way over to Fife, there is an outpost of light upon Inchkeith, and far to seaward, yet another on the May.

And while you are looking, across upon the Castle Hill, the drums and bugles begin to recall the scattered garrison; the air thrills with the sound; the bugles sing aloud; and the last rising flourish mounts and melts into the darkness like a star: a martial swan-song, fitly rounding in the labours of the day.

The Port of Leith

WINTER AND NEW YEAR

THE SCOTCH dialect is singularly rich in terms of reproach against the winter wind. *Snell, blae, nirly,* and *scowthering,* are four of these significant vocables; they are all words that carry a shiver with them; and for my part, as I see them aligned before me on the page, I am persuaded that a big wind comes tearing over the Firth from Burntisland and the northern hills; I think I can hear it howl in the chimney, and as I set my face northwards, feel its smarting kisses on my cheek. Even in the names of places there is often a desolate, inhospitable sound; and I remember two from the near neighbourhood of Edinburgh, Cauldhame and Blaw-weary, that would promise but starving comfort to their inhabitants. The inclemency of heaven, which has thus endowed the language of Scotland with words, has also largely modified the spirit of its poetry. Both poverty and a northern climate teach men the love of the hearth and the sentiment of the family: and the latter, in its own right, inclines a poet to the praise of strong waters. In Scotland, all our singers have a stave or two for blazing fires and stout potations:— to get indoors out of the wind and to swallow something hot to the stomach, are benefits so easily appreciated where they dwelt!

And this is not only so in country districts where the shepherd must wade in the snow all day after his flock, but in Edinburgh itself, and nowhere more apparently stated than in the works of our Edinburgh poet, Fergusson. He was a delicate youth, I take it, and willingly slunk from the robustious winter to an inn fireside. Love was absent from his life, or only present, if you prefer, in such a form that even the least serious of Burns's amourettes was ennobling by comparison; and so there is nothing to temper the sentiment of indoor revelry which pervades the poor boy's verses. Although it is characteristic of his native town, and the manners of its youth to the present day, this spirit has perhaps done something to restrict his popularity. He recalls a summer-party pleasantry with something akin to tenderness; and sounds the praises of the act of drinking as if it were virtuous, or at least witty, in itself. The kindly jar, the warm atmosphere of tavern parlours, and the revelry of lawyers' clerks, do not offer by themselves the materials of a rich existence. It was not choice, so much as an external fate, that kept Fergusson in this round of sordid pleasures. A Scot of poetic temperament, and without religious exaltation, drops as if by nature into the public-house. The picture may not be pleasing; but what else is a man to do in this dog's weather?

To none but those who have themselves suffered the thing in the body, can the gloom and depression of our Edinburgh winter be brought home. For some constitutions there is something almost physically disgusting in the bleak ugliness of easterly weather; the wind wearies, the sickly sky depresses them; and they turn back from their walk to avoid the aspect of the unrefulgent sun going down among perturbed and pallid mists. The days are so short that a man does much of his business, and certainly all his pleasure, by the haggard glare of gas lamps. The roads are as heavy as a fallow. People go by, so drenched and draggle-tailed that I have often wondered how they found the heart to undress. And meantime the wind whistles through the town as if it were an open meadow; and if you lie awake all night, you hear it shrieking and raving overhead with a noise of shipwrecks and of falling houses. In a word, life is so unsightly that there are times when the heart turns sick in a man's inside; and the look of a tavern, or the thought of the warm, fire-lit study, is like the touch of land to one who has been long struggling with the seas.

As the weather hardens towards frost, the world begins to improve for Edinburgh people. We enjoy superb, sub-arctic sunsets, with the profile of the city stamped in indigo upon a sky of luminous green. The wind may still be cold, but there is a briskness in the air that stirs good blood. People do not all look equally sour and downcast. They fall into two divisions; one, the knight of the blue face and hollow paunch, whom Winter has gotten by the vitals; the other well lined with New-year's fare, conscious of the touch of cold on his periphery, but stepping through it by the glow of his internal fires. Such an one I remember, triply cased in grease, whom no extremity of temperature could vanquish. 'Well,' would be his jovial salutation, 'here's a sneezer!' And the look of these warm fellows is tonic, and upholds their drooping fellow-townsmen. There is yet another class who do not depend on corporal advantages, but support the winter in virtue of a brave and merry heart. One shivering evening, cold enough for frost but with too high a wind, and a little past sundown, when the lamps were beginning to enlarge their circles in the growing dusk, a brace of barefoot lassies were seen coming eastward in the teeth of the wind. If the one was as much as nine, the other was certainly not more than seven. They were miserably clad; and the pavement was so cold, you would have thought no one could lay a naked foot on it unflinching. Yet they came along waltzing, if you please, while the elder sang a tune to give them music. The person who saw this, and whose heart was full of bitterness at the moment, pocketed a reproof which has been of use to him ever since, and which he now hands on, with his good wishes, to the reader.

At length, Edinburgh, with her satellite hills and all the sloping country, are sheeted up in white. If it has happened in the dark hours, nurses pluck their children out of bed and run with them to some commanding window, whence they may see the change that has been worked upon earth's face. 'A' the hills are covered wi' snaw,' they sing, 'and Winter's noo come fairly!' And the children, marvelling at the silence and the white landscape, find a spell appropriate to the season in the words. The reverberation of the snow increases the pale daylight, and brings all objects nearer the eye. The Pentlands are smooth and glittering, with here and there the black ribbon of a dry-stone dyke, and here and there, if there be wind, a cloud of blowing snow upon a shoulder.

The Firth seems a leaden creek, that a man might almost jump across, between well-powdered Lothian and well-powdered Fife. And the effect is not, as in other cities, a thing of half a day; the streets are soon trodden black, but the country keeps its virgin white; and you have only to lift your eyes and look over miles of country snow. An indescribable cheerfulness breathes about the city; and the well-fed heart sits lightly and beats gaily in the bosom. It is New-year's weather.

South Bridge Street

New-year's Day, the great national festival, is a time of family expansions and of deep carousal. Sometimes, by a sore stroke of fate for this Calvanistic people, the year's anniversary falls upon a Sunday, when the public-houses are inexorably closed, when singing and even whistling is banished from our homes and highways, and the oldest toper feels called upon to go to church. Thus pulled about, as if between two loyalties, the Scotch have to decide many nice cases of conscience, and ride the marches narrowly between the weekly and the annual observance. A party of convivial musicians, next door to a friend of mine, hung suspended in this manner on the brink of their diversions. From ten o'clock on Sunday night, my friend heard them tuning their instruments; and as the hour of liberty drew near, each must have had his music open, his bow in readiness across the fiddle, his foot already raised to mark the time, and his nerves braced for execution; for hardly had the twelfth stroke sounded from the earliest steeple, before they had launched forth into a secular bravura.

Currant-loaf is now popular eating in all households. For weeks before the great morning, confectioners display stacks of Scotch bun — a dense, black substance, inimical to life — and full moons of shortbread adorned with mottoes of peel or sugar-plum, in honour of the season and the family affections. 'Frae Auld Reekie,' 'A guid New Year to ye a', 'For the Auld Folk at Hame,' are among the most favoured of these devices. Can you not see the carrier, after half-a-day's journey on pinching hill-roads, draw up before a cottage in Teviotdale, or perhaps in Manor Glen among the rowans, and the old people receiving the parcel with moist eyes and a prayer for Jock or Jean in the city? For at this season, on the threshold of another year of calamity and stubborn conflict, men feel a need to draw closer the links that unite them; they reckon the number of their friends, like allies before a war; and the prayers grow longer in the morning as the absent are recommended by name into God's keeping.

On the day itself, the shops are all shut as on a Sunday; only taverns, toyshops, and other holiday magazines, keep open doors. Every one looks for his handsel. The postmen and the lamplighters have left, at every house in their districts, a copy of vernacular verses, asking and thanking in a breath; and it is characteristic of Scotland that these verses may have sometimes a touch of reality in detail or sentiment and a measure of strength in the handling. All over the town, you may see comforter'd schoolboys hasting to squander their half-crowns. There are an infinity of visits to be paid; all the world is in the street, except the daintier classes; the sacramental greeting is heard upon all sides; Auld Lang Syne is much in people's mouths; and whisky

New Year Celebration at the Tron Church

· 83 ·

and shortbread are staple articles of consumption. From an early hour a stranger will be impressed by the number of drunken men; and by afternoon, drunkenness has spread to the women. With some classes of society, it is as much a matter of duty to drink hard on New-Year's Day as to go to church on Sunday. Some have been saving their wages for perhaps a month to do the season honour. Many carry a whisky-bottle in their pocket, which they will press with embarrassing effusion on a perfect stranger. It is inexpedient to risk one's body in a cab, or not, at least, until after a prolonged study of the driver. The streets, which are thronged from end to end, become a place for delicate pilotage. Singly or arm-in-arm, some speechless, others noisy and quarrelsome, the votaries of the New Year go meandering in and out and cannoning one against another; and now and again, one falls and lies as he has fallen. Before night, so many have gone to bed or the police office, that the streets seem almost clearer. And as *guisards* and *first-footers* are now not much seen except in country places, when once the New Year has been rung in and proclaimed at the Tron railings, the festivities begin to find their way indoors and something like quiet returns upon the town. But think, in these piled *lands*, of all the senseless snorers, all the broken heads and empty pockets!

Of old, Edinburgh University was the scene of heroic snow-balling; and one riot obtained the epic honours of military intervention. But the great generation, I am afraid, is at an end; and even during my own college days, the spirit appreciably declined. Skating and sliding, on the other hand, are honoured more and more; and curling, being a creature of the national genius, is little likely to be disregarded. The patriotism that leads a man to eat Scotch bun will scarce desert him at the curling-pond. Edinburgh, with its long, steep pavements, is the proper home of sliders; many a happy urchin can slide the whole way to school; and the profession of errand boy is transformed into a holiday amusement. As for skating, there is scarce any city so handsomely provided. Duddingstone Loch lies under the abrupt southern side of Arthur's Seat; in summer, a shield of blue, with swans sailing from the reeds; in winter, a field of ringing ice. The

Duddingstone

village church sits above it on a green promontory; and the
village smoke rises from among goodly trees. At the church gates,
is the historical *joug*, a place of penance for the neck of detected
sinners, and the historical *louping-on stane*, from which Dutch-
built lairds and farmers climbed into the saddle. Here Prince
Charlie slept before the battle of Prestonpans; and here Deacon
Brodie, or one of his gang, stole a plough coulter before the
burglary in Chessel's Court. On the opposite side of the loch, the
ground rises to Craigmillar Castle, a place friendly to Stuart

Craigmillar Castle

Mariolaters. It is worth a climb, even in summer, to **look down** upon the loch from Arthur's Seat; but it is tenfold more so **on a** day of skating. The surface is thick with people moving easily and swiftly and leaning over at a thousand graceful inclinations; the crowd opens and closes, and keeps moving through itself like water; and the ice rings to half a mile away, with the flying steel. As night draws on, the single figures melt into the dusk, until only an obscure stir and coming and going of black clusters, is visible upon the loch. A little longer, and the first torch is kindled and begins to flit rapidly across the ice in a ring of yellow reflection, and this is followed by another and another, until the whole field is full of skimming lights.

Burns' Lodging, Buccleuch Pend

THE
PENTLAND
HILLS

ON THREE SIDES of Edinburgh, the country slopes
downward from the city, here to the sea, there to the fat
farms of Haddington, there to the mineral fields of Linlithgow.
On the south alone, it keeps rising until it not only out-tops the
Castle but looks down on Arthur's Seat. The character of the
neighbourhood is pretty strongly marked by a scarcity of hedges;
by many stone walls of varying height; by a fair amount of
timber, some of it well grown, but apt to be of a bushy, northern
profile and poor in foliage; by here and there a little river, Esk or
Leith or Almond, busily journeying in the bottom of its glen; and
from almost every point, by a peep of the sea or the hills. There is
no lack of variety, and yet most of the elements are common to all
parts; and the southern district is alone distinguished by
considerable summits and a wide view.

From Boroughmuirhead, where the Scottish army encamped
before Flodden, the road descends a long hill, at the bottom of
which and just as it is preparing to mount upon the other side, it
passes a toll-bar and issues at once into the open country. Even as
I write these words, they are being antiquated in the progress of
events, and the chisels are tinkling on a new row of houses. The
builders have at length adventured beyond the toll which held
them in respect so long, and proceed to career in these fresh
pastures like a herd of colts turned loose. As Lord Beaconsfield
proposed to hang an architect by way of stimulation, a man,
looking on these doomed meads, imagines a similar example to

deter the builders; for it seems as if it must come to an open fight at last to preserve a corner of green country unbedevilled. And here, appropriately enough, there stood in old days a crow-haunted gibbet, with two bodies hanged in chains. I used to be shown, when a child, a flat stone in the roadway to which the gibbet had been fixed. People of a willing fancy were persuaded, and sought to persuade others, that this stone was never dry. And no wonder, they would add, for the two men had only stolen fourpence between them.

For about two miles the road climbs upwards, a long hot walk in summer time. You reach the summit at a place where four ways meet, beside the toll of Fairmilehead. The spot is breezy and agreeable both in name and aspect. The hills are close by across a valley: Kirk Yetton, with its long, upright scars visible as far as Fife, and Allermuir the tallest on this side: with wood and tilled field running high upon their borders, and haunches all moulded into innumerable glens and shelvings and variegated with heather and fern. The air comes briskly and sweetly off the hills, pure from the elevation and rustically scented by the upland plants; and even at the toll, you may hear the curlew calling on its mate. At certain seasons, when the gulls desert their surfy forelands, the birds of sea and mountain hunt and scream together in the same field by Fairmilehead. The winged, wild things intermix their wheelings, the seabirds skim the tree tops and fish among the furrows of the plough. These little craft of air are at home in all the world, so long as they cruise in their own element; and like sailors, ask but food and water from the shores they coast.

Below, over a stream, the road passes Bow Bridge, now a dairy-farm, but once a distillery of whisky. It chanced, some time in the past century, that the distiller was on terms of good-fellowship with the visiting officer of excise. The latter was of an easy, friendly disposition and a master of convivial arts. Now and again, he had to walk out of Edinburgh to measure the distiller's stock; and although it was agreeable to find his business lead him in a friend's direction, it was unfortunate that the friend should be a loser by his visits. Accordingly, when he got about the level of Fairmilehead, the gauger would take his flute, without which he never travelled, from his pocket, fit it together, and set manfully to playing, as if for his own delectation and inspired by the beauty of the scene. His favourite air, it seems, was 'Over the hills and far away.' At the first note, the distiller pricked his ears. A flute at Fairmilehead? and playing 'Over the hills and far away?' This must be his friendly enemy, the gauger. Instantly, horses were harnessed, and sundry barrels of whisky were got upon a cart, driven at a gallop round Hill End, and buried in the mossy glen behind Kirk Yetton. In the same breath, you may be sure, a fat fowl was put to the fire, and the whitest napery prepared for the back parlour. A little after, the gauger, having had his fill of music for the moment, came strolling down with the most innocent air imaginable, and found the good people at Bow Bridge taken entirely unawares by his arrival, but none the less glad to see him. The distiller's liquor and the gauger's flute would combine to speed the moments of digestion; and when both were somewhat mellow, they would wind up the evening with 'Over the hills and far away' to an accompaniment of knowing glances. And at least, there is a smuggling story, with original and half-idyllic features.

A little further, the road to the right passes an upright stone in a field. The country people call it General Kay's monument. According to them, an officer of that name had perished there in battle at some indistinct period before the beginning of history. The date is reassuring; for I think cautious writers are silent on the General's exploits. But the stone is connected with one of those remarkable tenures of land which linger on into the modern world from Feudalism. Whenever the reigning sovereign passes by, a certain landed proprietor is held bound to climb on to the top, trumpet in hand, and sound a flourish according to the measure of his knowledge in that art. Happily for a respectable family, crowned heads have no great business in the Pentland Hills. But the story lends a character of comicality to the stone; and the passer-by will sometimes chuckle to himself.

The district is dear to the superstitious. Hard by, at the backgate of Comiston, a belated carter beheld a lady in white 'with the most beautiful, clear shoes upon her feet,' who looked upon him in a very ghastly manner and then vanished; and just in front is the Hunters' Tryst, once a roadside inn, and not so long ago haunted by the devil in person. Satan led the inhabitants a pitiful existence. He shook the four corners of the building with lamentable outcries, beat at the doors and windows, overthrew crockery in the dead hours of the morning, and danced unholy dances on the roof. Every kind of spiritual disinfectant was put in requisition; chosen ministers were summoned out of Edinburgh and prayed by the hour; pious neighbours sat up all night making a noise of psalmody; but Satan minded them no more than the wind about the hill-tops; and it was only after years of persecution, that he left the Hunter's Tryst in peace to occupy himself with the remainder of mankind. What with General Kay, and the white lady, and this singular visitation, the neighbourhood offers great facilities to the makers of sun-myths; and without exactly casting in one's lot with that disenchanting school of writers, one cannot help hearing a good deal of the winter wind in the last story. 'That nicht,' says Burns, in one of his happiest moments, —

> 'That nicht a child might understand
> The deil had business on his hand.'

And if people sit up all night in lone places on the hills, with Bibles and tremulous psalms, they will be apt to hear some of the most fiendish noises in the world: the wind will beat on doors and dance upon roofs for them, and make the hills howl around their cottage with a clamour like the judgment-day.

The road goes down through another valley, and then finally begins to scale the main slope of the Pentlands. A bouquet of old trees stands round a white farm-house; and from a neighbouring dell, you can see smoke rising and leaves ruffling in the breeze. Straight above, the hills climb a thousand feet into the air. The neighbourhood, about the time of lambs, is clamorous with the bleating of flocks; and you will be wakened, in the grey of early summer mornings, by the barking of a dog or the voice of a shepherd shouting to the echoes. This, with the hamlet lying behind unseen, is Swanston.

Swanston Cottage, where the Stevenson family had a summer home

The place in the dell is immediately connected with the city. Long ago, this sheltered field was purchased by the Edinburgh magistrates for the sake of the springs that rise or gather there. After they had built their waterhouse and laid their pipes, it occurred to them that the place was suitable for junketing. Once entertained, with jovial magistrates and public funds, the idea led speedily to accomplishment; and Edinburgh could soon boast of a municipal Pleasure House. The dell was turned into a garden; and on the knoll that shelters it from the plain and the sea winds, they built a cottage looking to the hills. They brought crockets and gargoyles from old St Giles's which they were then restoring, and disposed them on the gables and over the door and about the garden; and the quarry which had supplied them with building material, they draped with clematis and carpeted with beds of roses. So much for the pleasure of the eye; for creature comfort, they made a capacious cellar in the hillside and fitted it with bins of the hewn stone. In process of time, the trees grew higher and gave shade to the cottage, and the evergreens sprang up and turned the dell into a thicket. There, purple magistrates relaxed themselves from the pursuit of municipal ambition; cocked hats paraded soberly about the garden and in and out among the hollies; authoritative canes drew ciphering upon the walk; and at night, from high upon the hills, a shepherd saw lighted windows through the foliage and heard the voice of city dignitaries raised in song.

The farm is older. It was first a grange of Whitekirk Abbey, tilled and inhabited by rosy friars. Thence, after the Reformation, it passed into the hands of a true-blue Protestant family. During the covenanting troubles, when a night conventicle was held upon the Pentlands, the farm doors stood hospitably open till the morning; the dresser was laden with cheese and bannocks, milk and brandy; and the worshippers kept slipping down from the hill between two exercises, as couples visit the supper-room between two dances of a modern ball. In the Forty-five, some foraging Highlanders from Prince Charlie's army fell upon Swanston in the dawn. The great-grandfather of the late farmer was then a little child; him they awakened by plucking the blankets from his bed, and he remembered, when he was an old man, their truculent looks and uncouth speech. The churn stood full of cream in the dairy, and with this they made their brose in high delight. 'It was braw brose,' said one of them. At last, they made off, laden like camels with their booty; and Swanston Farm has lain out of the way of history from that time forward. I do not know what may be yet in store for it. On dark days, when the mist runs low upon the hill, the house has a gloomy air as if suitable for private tragedy. But in hot July, you can fancy nothing more perfect than the garden, laid out in alleys and arbours and bright, old-fashioned flower-plots, and ending in a miniature ravine, all trellis-work and moss and tinkling waterfall, and housed from the sun under fathoms of broad foliage.

The hamlet behind is one of the least considerable of hamlets, and consists of a few cottages on a green beside a burn. Some of them (a strange thing in Scotland) are models of internal neatness; the beds adorned with patchwork, the shelves arrayed with willow-pattern plates, the floors and tables bright with scrubbing or pipeclay, and the very kettle polished like silver. It is the sign of a contented old age in country places, where there is little matter for gossip and no street sights. Housework becomes an art; and at evening, when the cottage interior shines and twinkles in the glow of the fire, the housewife folds her hands and contemplates her finished picture; the snow and the wind may do their worst, she has made herself a pleasant corner in the world. The city might be a thousand miles away: and yet it was from close by that Mr Bough painted the distant view of Edinburgh which has been etched for this collection: and you have only to look at the plate, to see how near it is at hand. But hills and hill people are not easily sophisticated; and if you walk out here on a summer Sunday, it is as like as not the shepherd may set his dogs upon you. But keep an unmoved countenance; they look formidable at the charge, but their hearts are in the right place; and they will only bark and sprawl about you on the grass, unmindful of their master's excitations.

Kirk Yetton forms the north-eastern angle of the range; thence, the Pentlands trend off to south and west. From the summit you look over a great expense of champaign sloping to the sea and behold a large variety of distant hills. There are the hills of Fife, the hills of Peebles, the Lammermoors and the Ochils, more or less mountainous in outline, more or less blue with distance. Of the Pentlands themselves, you see a field of wild heathery peaks with a pond gleaming in the midst; and to that side the view is as desolate as if you were looking into Galloway or Applecross. To turn to the other, is like a piece of travel. Far out in the lowlands Edinburgh shows herself, making a great smoke on clear days and spreading her suburbs about her for miles; the Castle rises darkly in the midst; and close by, Arthur's Seat makes a bold figure in the landscape. All around, cultivated fields, and woods, and smoking villages, and white country roads, diversify the uneven surface of the land. Trains crawl slowly abroad upon the railway lines; little ships are tacking in the Firth; the shadow of a mountainous cloud, as large as a parish, travels before the wind; the wind itself ruffles the wood and standing corn, and sends pulses of varying colour across the landscape. So you sit, like Jupiter upon Olympus, and look down from afar

Distant View of Edinburgh (Etching by Sam Bough, R.S.A., from the original edition) upon men's life. The city is as silent as a city of the dead: from all its humming thoroughfares, not a voice, not a footfall, reaches you upon the hill. The sea surf, the cries of ploughmen, the streams and the mill-wheels, the birds and the wind, keep up an animated concert through the plain; from farm to farm, dogs and crowing cocks contend together in defiance; and yet from this Olympian station, except for the whispering rumour of a train, the world has fallen into a dead silence, and the business of town and country grown voiceless in your ears. A crying hill-bird, the bleat of a sheep, a wind singing in the dry grass, seem not so much to interrupt, as to accompany, the stillness; but to the spiritual ear, the whole scene makes a music at once human and rural and discourses pleasant reflections on the destiny of man. The spiry habitable city, ships, the divided fields, and browsing herds, and the straight highways, tell visibly of man's active and comfortable ways; and you may be never so laggard and never so unimpressionable, but there is something in the view that spirits up your blood and puts you in the vein for cheerful labour.

Immediately below is Fairmilehead, a spot of roof and a smoking chimney, where two roads, no thicker than packthread, intersect beside a hanging wood. If you are fanciful, you will be reminded of the gauger in the story. And the thought of this old exciseman, who once lipped and fingered on his pipe and uttered clear notes from it in the mountain air, and the words of the song he affected, carry your mind 'Over the hills and far away' to distant countries; and you have a vision of Edinburgh not, as you see her, in the midst of a little neighbourhood, but as a boss upon the round world with all Europe and the deep sea for her surroundings. For every place is a centre to the earth, whence highways radiate or ships set sail for foreign ports; the limit of a parish is not more imaginary than the frontier of an empire; and as a man sitting at home in his cabinet and swiftly writing books, so a city sends abroad an influence and a portrait of herself. There is no Edinburgh emigrant, far or near, from China to Peru, but he or she carries some lively pictures of the mind, some sunset behind the Castle cliffs, some snow scene, some maze of city lamps, indelible in the memory and delightful to study in the intervals of toil. For any such, if this book fall in their way, here are a few more home pictures. It would be pleasant, if they should recognise a house where they had dwelt or a walk that they had taken.

PUBLISHER'S POSTSCRIPT

ALTHOUGH Edinburgh is still one of the most attractive cities in the world, the reader must not expect to find every one of the places pictured still in existence. The city fathers have been less than sensible of their heritage, and the depredation has been going on a long time. Architects and their usually wealthy institutional clients, much more concerned with pelf than posterity, have mangled unity by interpolating totally unsuitable buildings, the most marked example being the modern St James' Centre which, while no doubt convenient for shoppers, caused the destruction of the unique Continental-looking aspect of Leith Street shown in Hanslip Fletcher's drawing on page 62. The new building, obtrusively prominent from Calton Hill, thrusts its bulk upon the cityscape like a hideous toad. Paces away, Sir Arthur Conan Doyle's birthplace was razed in 1969 to make way for a roundabout on which was erected an absurdity so alien to the historical beauty of Edinburgh that Stevenson would undoubtedly have had a wry comment about it, though he would not have easily believed it either.

As long ago as 1911 James Bone in *Edinburgh Revisited* was recording that there had been "talk of destroying Charlotte Square," which is one of the finest architectural gems of Britain, though in Stevenson's time the New Town was not universally liked. Happily Charlotte Square is still unspoiled, which cannot be said in respect of St Andrew's Square, unnecessarily ruined by inappropriate redevelopment.

No city can escape change, but planners should pay more heed to the patina of time and the appropriateness of new buildings among old edifices. The renovation of the Canongate has been hailed as masterly, but surely how much more suitable would it have been to retain more of the old façades?

In common with other historic places like Chester, Bath and Cambridge, to name a few which have blighted their heritage, Edinburgh continues to permit insensitive alterations, and is a very different place from that which R.L.S. knew. All of the illustrations in this edition are, however, facets of his own city of birth which he would have recognised, and which, in spite of everything, you, dear Reader, may in many instances yet see for yourself.